THE
TERRIBLE
TRUTH
ABOUT INVESTING

The
TERRIBLE
TRUTH
ABOUT INVESTING

HOW TO BE
A SAVVY INVESTOR

Bruce J. Temkin, MSPA, EA

Foreword by Don Phillips
President of Morningstar, Inc.

Edited by Deborah L. Thomas, JD, CFP

Fairfield Press
2900 Fourth Street North, Suite A202
St. Petersburg, FL 33704
Phone: 888-820-5958   Fax: 727-821-1713

Printed in the United States of America
10 9 8 7 6 5 4 3 2 1

ISBN: 0-9665873-0-8
Library of Congress Catalog Number: 98-93827

Source for the following charts and tables: © *Stocks, Bonds, Bills & Inflation 1997 Yearbook*[TM], Ibbotson Associates, Chicago (annually updated work by Roger G. Ibbotson and Rex Sinquefield). Used with permission. All rights reserved.

Charts: 2-2, 2-3, 2-4, 2-5, 2-6, 2-7, all charts in chapter 5, 6-2, 6-3, 7-4,
7-6, 8-1

Tables: 4-5, 4-6, 4-7, 4-8, 6-3, 6-7, 7-1, 7-3, 7-4

Source for Morningstar reports: Morningstar, Inc. All rights reserved. 225 W. Wacker Dr., Chicago IL 60606. Although data are gathered from reliable sources, Morningstar cannot guarantee completeness and accuracy. Used with permission.

This publication is designed to provide accurate and authoritative information in regard to the subject matter covered. It is sold with the understanding that neither the author nor the publsher is engaged in rendering legal, accounting or other professional service. If investment or other expert assistance is required, the services of a competent professional person should be sought. *From a Declaration of Principles jointly adopted by a Committee of the American Bar Association and a Committee of Publishers.*

To my loving wife Kate and our son Patrick.
As I told Patrick,
"Dad tried his very best."

ACKNOWLEDGMENTS

This book has come from the influences throughout my life of literally hundreds of people that have encouraged me in various ways, from individuals that have shown generosity and kindness, to scholars that I have taught with or read. This list is so vast. I would like to name a few here, and in my next book, name more. Pauline and Ted Temkin, Beverly and Knight Travis, Beven Alvey, Sandy and Harold Apolinsky, John Becker, Roger and Judy Benson, Bill Berry, Patricia Brown, Paula Calimafde, Natalie Choate, Tom Connelly, Michael Coyne, Berrien Eaton, Robert Elkus, Adelle Franz, Michael Granfield, Morton Harris, Zoe Hicks, Diane Hume, Tom Joseph, Mike Kaplan, Louis Kravitz, Harry Lamon, William Lieber, Alson Martin, Greg Matthews, Donald Maclay, John Merkle, Essie and Leonard Neff, William Raby, John Stoessinger, Patrick Suffern, Robert Taichert, all my friends in The Group, and my fellow board members at The Center for Infant/Parent Development, and Small Business Council of America.

I am particularly grateful to Roger Gibson and Harold Evensky, who not only helped me better understand but also inspired my interest in the field of investing.

I would also like to thank the countless organizations over the last 25 years—including business, civic, charitable, investment and financial, legal and accounting symposiums throughout the United states—that have sought me out as a speaker and given me the opportunity to express my ideas and educational materials.

There were a number of individuals that specifically helped me put these ideas into print. My good friend and colleague Deborah L. Thomas with Silver Oak Advisory Group, gave countless hours far beyond the call of duty, providing technical contributions, editing, research, and brainstorming of ideas. Her sense of humor, generosity, encouragement and tireless ability to keep me focused were critical in getting this book finished. W. Scott Simon was a great help with research and contributions, including several readings of the manuscript with expert criticism and editorial suggestions. The following people also made contributions to this text and have my deepest appreciation: Mike Hadow, Guerdon Ely and Tom Connelly for their technical review and observations, Paul Braghero for graphics, and a very special thank you to Maron Moses.

Once the book was finished, my wife Kate turned to me and said, "Imprimatur Nihil Obstat."

Foreword

by Don Phillips
The Terrible Truth About Investing

Investing at its heart is a simple activity. Buy low and sell high are not hard lessons to grasp, but they can be exceedingly difficult to execute. Unfortunately, in an attempt to get down to investment basics, too many of us cling to simplistic measures such as buy, sell, or hold recommendations, or, yes, even Morningstar's star ratings. These measures are neither good nor bad by themselves, but if they become a surrogate for exercising judgment, then their simple appeal can lead to something other than optimum investment choices. If an investor is to use these tools wisely he or she must understand their construction and their limits, which is why we at Morningstar have always been completely candid about how and why we construct our star ratings.

One of the overriding limitations of all investment research is that it focuses on the only available variable, the investment. Yet, many of the most critical questions one can ask in making a successful investment are about the investor, not the investment. We should think of investments not in the simplistic terms of good or bad, but as appropriate or inappropriate for a given individual in a given situation. Moreover, even as we employ academic teachings or new technologies to aid us in the investment process, we must not forget the art, the interpretation, the exercise of judgment about what historical analysis both does and doesn't tell us.

Bruce Temkin's *The Terrible Truth About Investing* addresses exactly these issues. It is the right book at the right time from the right author. Bruce's detailed understanding of the academic arguments shaping our investment decision making is unparalleled. But that alone would not make this the wonderful book that it is. Bruce's true gift is his understanding of human behavior and his intense compassion for investors and advisors. This book isn't about self-aggrandizement or the promotion of one investment approach over another. Instead, it is that rarest of all investment texts, one written from the heart with one pure purpose—to help investors make better investment decisions.

As the desire to help investors has been the guiding spirit behind Morningstar, I feel a great affinity for this text. It tackles complex topics in a straightforward, but never simplistic, fashion. Moreover, because it focuses on vital investment principles, such as our understanding of risk, it is a book that rewards all readers, from beginning investors to experienced advisors. These terrible truths require ample study. For while some are deceptively easy to grasp, they are all incredibly difficult to master. I hope sincerely that this book is read and reread for many years to come.

Don Phillips
President, Morningstar, Inc.
Chicago, Illinois

Table of Contents

Temkin's Observations

PREFACE

Not long ago, a good friend asked for some advice concerning investment decisions he needed to make regarding his 401(k) plan and other personal assets. He said that he had read several books on how to invest but was still not sure of what he should do. I told him that he was trying to make critical investment decisions without first acquiring the necessary background, like trying to run before learning to walk. I suggested that we go to a bookstore and look for books that focused not on how to invest, but stressed the investment principles that would give him the foundation all investors need before making critical investment decisions.

That afternoon we visited several bookstores. I was troubled not to find any books with in-depth discussions of such essential issues as real rates of return, investment time horizons, and risk and volatility. I was even more troubled to discover that, while many of the books available discussed the history of investment returns, they ignored investor's behavior. I saw isolated discussions of important principles, but the books only supplied pieces of a puzzle, not the complete picture I had hoped to find. My disappointment in not finding the type of information my friend needed triggered my desire to write this book on investment principles.

While writing this book, I asked a number of sophisticated investment advisors and financial planners to review the manuscript to determine whether I was achieving my goal of providing investment principles to individual investors. The reaction of these investment professionals was that not only could this book help individual investors, it would also help advisors better communicate important investment principles with which even their most sophisticated clients struggle.

When people ask me why I named this book *The Terrible Truth About Investing*, I answer that investing is an incredibly complex discipline over the long term. In addition, the very principles we must rely on in order to deal with its complexities are being vastly over-simplified or even ignored.

INTRODUCTION: BECOMING A SAVVY INVESTOR

Never in history have so many millions of individuals been required to make critical investment decisions. The Federal Reserve reported that at the year's end 1990, individuals directly or indirectly owned investments worth $3.1 trillion. By the year-end 1997 that total was $11.4 trillion. The challenge to invest those assets well is complicated by the fact that individuals will be responsible for making investment decisions for unprecedented periods of time. The ability to make savvy investment decisions will play a decisive role in achieving key financial goals, such as the ability to retire comfortably, funding a child's education, considering alternative careers or the opportunity to work less.

Many factors contribute to the need to become a savvy investor: the tremendous growth of 401(k) retirement plans and IRAs, the questionable future viability of Social Security and Medicare, a shift away from traditional defined-benefit pension plans, job instability and longer life expectancies, and these are just the "tip of the iceberg."

Unfortunately, many investors do not understand the basic investment principles necessary to make wise choices. If any one principle is overlooked, it may be only a matter of time before even a well-thought-out investment strategy collapses. This is why you need to be a "savvy" investor.

Webster defines *savvy* as "common sense, practical understanding, knowledge, sensible." Being a savvy investor—whether you make your own investment decisions, use mutual funds or hire an investment advisor—not only requires understanding and applying the principles but also constantly re-examining them. The ability to do this can increase your chances of becoming a successful long-term investor.

In this book, we will explore a broad spectrum of principles that are essential to investment decision making. This inquiry will lead us into a number of areas—some whose bearing on investing will be obvious while others will be a complete surprise. Among the topics we will examine are a history of investment returns, diversification, risk and volatility, life-cycle investing, and using computers to make investment decisions. In addition, we will make observations about what may be the most overlooked factor in being a savvy investor: the powerful role that *human nature and real-life experiences* play in investing.

It is important that investment information, history, and principles are examined side by side with the personal and emotional experiences investors encounter over the course of their lives. Otherwise, the very principles we must rely upon can be distorted or oversimplified.

Following are some of the investment issues and principles that savvy investors know and use in their decision making.

Savvy investors...

- Not only are aware of the advantages of diversification, but—more importantly—understand what they give up to get those benefits.

- Know why frequently used investment charts, tables and educational materials often are misinterpreted.

- Know what essential questions are _not_ being asked on risk tolerance questionnaires.

- Are concerned with their personal inflation rates, not with the government's stated inflation rate.

- Understand that the _real_ rate of return of an investment is important, not its _stated_ rate of return.

- Understand why many institutional investors abandoned their investment policies during prolonged down stock markets.

- Understand why they must examine the risk and return characteristics of each investment in their portfolios.

- Are keenly aware of the planning limitations of investment and retirement planning software.

- Understand why lifecycle and age-based portfolio allocations are overly simplified.

- Understand the critical difference between statistical history and behavioral history.

- Are always aware if their investment advisors or mutual fund managers change investment strategies.

- Are aware that tax inefficiencies can result when investing their personal and retirement assets.

- Are aware of the most recent research on longevity and how it is crucial to investing through retirement.

- Know they can benefit from diversification, even in years when investments decline in value.

Some investors want to *become* savvy, while sophisticated investors and advisors desire to *remain* savvy. To accomplish either of these objectives requires both the recognition and continuous reexamination of the investment principles contained in this book.

INVESTMENT FUNDAMENTALS AND HISTORICAL RETURNS

Some Terrible Truths

- Investing is uncertain and unpredictable.

- Most investors don't know where investment performance comes from.

- Buying stocks can be like volunteering for combat.

- Statistical returns seldom reflect what investors actually earn.

- Many investors choose their investments without sufficient research into investment history.

Making Investment Decisions

How do we make investment decisions? Often, we follow the advice of a co-worker, relative or friend. We may read a magazine article or hear an "expert" on a TV or radio show. Or we might rely on information from providers of 401(k) plans, investment newsletters and books, professional advisors, investment seminars, computer software, or the Internet.

Confronted with so many investment options, strategies and choices, some investors feel overwhelmed. Often investors believe they have found solutions that simplify the process only to be disappointed. Decisions about investing money sometimes seem almost too difficult to make. The best way for investors to equip themselves for decision making is if they return to the basics: a fundamental understanding of investment principles, recent research, and the history of investment performance.

Fundamentals are essential in any endeavor. Baseball's spring training is a good example. Each year, even the most experienced veterans get together with the rookies and start from scratch. They stretch, warm up, take batting practice—they return to basics—to prepare for the upcoming season.

Investors, too, can improve their chances of making well-informed long-term decisions and reduce their chances of making costly errors by constantly returning to basic principles. This is true whether they make their own investment decisions or rely on advisors. All prospective investors need to understand and review certain investment fundamentals regardless of the investment strategy they use.

As we review different fundamentals we will also discuss what may be the most overlooked factor in investing: understanding *the relationship between statistical history and an investor's own unique personal history.* When we see historical returns we will discover that many, if not most, investors did not earn these historical returns. We will also look at a study that evaluated how the behavior of investors influenced their long-term performance.

Investment history can be viewed in different ways. For example, many investors believe they understand investment history because they have either seen, experienced or read about the stock market crash of October 1987 when the Dow Jones Industrial average (the Dow) dropped 508 points and lost more than 20 percent of its value in one day. However, the down market that accompanied this crash lasted only 90 days—which spared investors the battering of a falling stock market, where investors can take a pounding month-in and month-out for years. In fact, U.S. investors who have been in the market only since 1975 have not really lived through the trauma and brutality of a true prolonged down stock market.

In This Chapter...

A knowledge of investment history provides us the insights and perspectives we need to improve our chances of making appropriate investment decisions. We can begin to understand investment fundamentals by reviewing an important study that analyzed the investment returns of portfolios and assessed the roles played by market timing, security selection and portfolio design in earning those returns. Also, we will explore how financial markets have changed in recent years, and compare the characteristics of various types of investments or asset classes.

To review the history of investment performance, we'll refer to a landmark study that was first published in the mid-1970s. This research, updated annually, quantifies the rates of return for U.S. stocks, bonds and inflation since 1925. It provides the foundation for a variety of investment work that we see reported in articles, publications and educational material. Prior to this comprehensive study, little information on investment history was readily available to investors.

Once you have developed a better understanding of historical investment returns and the basic characteristics of asset classes, you will be in a better position to ask yourself this critical question: *when making investment decisions, will I rely on investment history to repeat itself?* How you answer this question may be one of the most important factors in your long-term investment performance. In later chapters, which explore other investment principles and issues, you will see how this question is much more complex than you might think.

Today's Investment World

Today's investment world differs radically from the past. In the mid-1970s, most money was invested directly by individuals. But by the mid-1990s, a major shift had occurred. Professional institutional investors such as mutual fund managers, investment bankers, pension fund managers, and insurance companies were making most investments.

These changes coincided with a remarkable growth of mutual funds—pools of money from numerous small and large investors. When people invest money in a mutual fund, a professional money manager uses it to purchase stocks or bonds of different companies, and the fund issues shares to its investors. In 1975 only 426 mutual funds existed, with a total of $45.9 billion invested in them. Today there are about 8,000 funds—more than there are stocks listed on the entire New York Stock Exchange—and new funds become available every day. Mutual fund investments were $1.0 trillion in 1990, exceeded $4.0 trillion by 1998, and continue to grow at a staggering rate.

Institutional Investing — But Personal Responsibility Remains

Even though we have seen a significant shift from individual investing to institutional investing, this is only a part of the picture. There has also been a tremendous movement from defined benefit pension plans to individually directed 401(k)s, IRAs and other tax-deferred retirement plans. Much of this money is invested in mutual funds. But even though these billions of dollars are then invested by mutual fund managers, it is individual investors who remain responsible for deciding which funds to choose.

Recent Investment Research

A study was published in 1986 by three investment analysts, Gary Brinson, Randolph Hood, and Gilbert Beebower entitled *Determinants of Portfolio Performance* (the Brinson Study). It examined the returns of 91 large pension funds in this country from 1974 through 1983 to determine the primary factors that influenced the variability of returns among these pension plans. The pension funds—many of them investing billions of dollars at the direction of some of the best money managers in the world—focused on long-term performance because they were investing retirement assets. A follow-up study in 1991 updated the research, and work by other analysts has also supplemented it. Although the Brinson Study looked at institutional pension funds, its conclusions are relevant for individual investors as they make investment decisions.

The study first identified three primary factors that could influence the overall performance of a portfolio: market timing, security selection, and portfolio design (or asset allocation). Next they determined how the variability of the funds' returns was influenced by these three factors over a 10-year period. Let's review each of the strategies examined by the Brinson Study, and then discuss its conclusions.

Market Timing

At the heart of a *market timing* strategy is the belief that one can accurately forecast up and down movements in the stock and bond markets. A market timer attempts to shift investments among stocks, bonds, cash, or other assets before the market moves in the anticipated direction. The market timer strives to buy a particular asset before it goes up, and to sell it before it goes down. The ability to accurately forecast these movements and then act accordingly favorably influences a portfolio's returns.

For a moment, assume you are a market timer. You have diligently researched the stock market. On the basis of your research, you conclude that the market is overvalued and that a downturn is just around the corner, so you sell your stocks and put the money into cash or bonds while you wait for the "corrective" drop in stock prices to occur. Later when you believe the stock market is about to go up, you move your money back into stocks.

Many researchers have concluded that successfully timing stock or bond markets over a long period of time is exceedingly difficult. The stock market in particular can move quickly and suddenly. In fact, a significant percentage of the stock market's returns for an entire year may come in a single month or even a single day.

If you had invested during the decade from 1980 to 1990 in the S&P 500 Index, which consists of the stocks of 500 of the largest publicly traded corporations in America (such as AT&T, Exxon, Proctor & Gamble, and General Electric), you would have earned an average annual compound return of 17.5 percent. But look at what would have happened if you had missed some of the best days during that 10-year period.

Between 1980 and 1990, the stock markets were open for trading for 2,528 days. Table 2-1 shows what would have happened to your 17.5 percent return if you had missed only the 10, 20, 30, or 40 best days out of the 2,528 total. The table also shows in each case how much $10,000 invested in the S&P 500 on the first day of 1980 would have been worth on the last day of 1989.

Table 2-1
Impact of Missed Trading Days from 1980–1990

Number of Best Days Missed	Average Annual Compound Return	Growth of $10,000 after Ten Years
None	17.5%	$56,820
10	12.7%	$35,370
20	9.6%	$26,010
30	8.9%	$24,270
40	4.4%	$15,510

As you can see, if you had simply invested $10,000 in the S&P 500 at the beginning of 1980 and did not sell, your investment would have grown to $56,820 by the end of 1989. But if you had attempted to time the market and happened to miss only the 10 best trading days for the 10-year period (less than one-half of 1 percent of all trading days), your average annual return would have fallen from 17.5 percent to 12.7 percent. If you had missed only the best 40 days of trading (just over 1.5 percent of the available trading days), your $10,000 would have been worth $15,510—a puny 4.4 percent average annual compound rate of return—over the full ten years.

(On the other hand, if you had managed to miss the 40 *worst* trading days in that decade, your total return would have been higher than if you had held onto the investment for the full ten years of ups and downs.)

Markets by their nature make sharp, quick, and random up and down movements. You can participate in these unpredictable movements only if you are invested in the market *before* they occur. Most investors who use market timing attempt to get out before a market falls. But you can suffer severely for missing the very beginning of a rising market or the best trading days. Market timers must attempt to make two correct forecasts: when to leave and when to reenter the market.

Security Selection

Another strategy studied by Brinson and his colleagues was *security selection*—picking stocks or bonds that investors believe will increase in value. A manager might look for a particular industry or stock that either seems ready for a period of growth or seems undervalued; simultaneously, the manager also tries to avoid stocks that seem overvalued. A manager's skill at picking good stocks or bonds and avoiding bad ones of course influences the portfolio's returns.

Picture 1,000 investment firms all over the county, all staffed with the best and brightest financial analysts, statisticians, and MBAs coming from the finest business schools. They research markets, individual companies, and economic information, and are aided by the most sophisticated computer modeling tools available. All of these organizations, in a world with immediate access to the same financial information, separately analyze *the same stocks and bonds.* The managers within these organizations buy and sell billions of dollars' worth of stocks and bonds every day.

Think about this. For a stock trade to occur, two people must agree on a price. For example, at the same moment that one investment professional thinks it is time to sell shares of General Electric, another investment professional thinks it is time to buy those same shares. Thus, markets have become a daily auction attended by sophisticated bidders. This highly competitive process leads to what some people call "an efficient market," meaning that the stocks are fairly priced.

> ### Stock and Art Auctions
>
> Stock trading can be compared to auctions of paintings, antiques or other collectibles. If only one knowledgeable collector shows up at the auction, she might be able to buy valuable antiques for bargain prices. But if many knowledgeable bidders attend, the antique is more likely to sell for a price reflecting its true value.

Portfolio Design

The third factor the Brinson Study identified was overall *portfolio design*, which has two components. First, a decision must be made as to which kinds of investments to use as building blocks for a portfolio. Among those available are stocks, bonds, cash, precious metals, real estate, stocks issued by international corporations and bonds issued by foreign governments.

Second, the portfolio manager must decide how to allocate or mix the various investments in the portfolio. One pension fund might have 60 percent of its total assets invested in U.S. stocks, 30 percent in U.S. bonds and 10 percent in cash. Another one might have 40 percent in U.S. stocks, 25 percent in U.S. bonds, 20 percent in international stocks, 10 percent in international bonds and 5 percent in cash. This decision process is often referred to as *asset allocation*. Portfolio design—the investments selected and the way they are allocated within a portfolio—affects the portfolio's overall performance.

The Results of the Brinson Study

Of the three factors studied—market timing, security selection, and portfolio design—which plays the most important role in determining variation of long-term portfolio returns? Most individual investors believe security selection is the most significant factor, and that market timing and portfolio design are less important. Others mention the influence of such factors as: the economy, expectations of interest rates, levels of inflation, corporate earnings, the party in control of the White House, Defense Department spending, Paris hemlines, the football conference that wins the Super Bowl, and other unusual investment factors, some bordering on the occult.

The actual results of the Brinson Study, as shown in Chart 2-1, indicate that more than 90 percent of the variability of the portfolios' performances during the study period was directly attributable to *the portfolio's design*. The Brinson Study further found that security selection accounted for less than 5 percent of the variabilities in return, while less than 2 percent could be attributed to market timing.

Why? In a world where most of the invested money is controlled by highly skilled professional money managers competing against each other, and because they are so good at what they do, it has become increasingly difficult for one to get an advantage over another.

While many investment professionals question how the Brinson Study reached its conclusions, and others question the percentages assigned to the determinants, what should not be doubted is the critical importance of portfolio design to long-term portfolio performance.

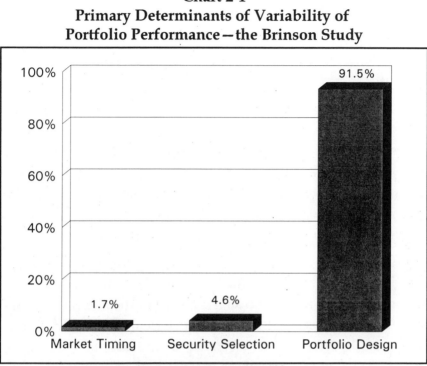

Chart 2-1
Primary Determinants of Variability of
Portfolio Performance—the Brinson Study

Note: numbers do not add to 100.

Investment Alternatives: Lending Versus Owning

The Brinson Study and other research have concluded that portfolio design has an overwhelmingly influence on long-term performance. But what investment alternatives can go into a portfolio design? When you buy a car, you wouldn't make a final decision without first comparing the kinds of cars for sale, the options available, the gas mileage you can expect, the price, and numerous other factors. So let's do some investment "tire kicking" by reviewing basic investment choices, the historical performance of major classes of investments, and their characteristics.

For the moment, let's assume you know absolutely nothing about investing. The first thing that might be explained to you involves the most basic choice of what you can do with your money: you can be a lender or an owner. Historically, lending and owning have had distinct investment characteristics and patterns of returns and risk.

Lending

Investors who choose to lend let other people use their money (borrow it) in return for receiving interest. For example, investors lend their money through securities such as certificates of deposit (CDs), corporate bonds, government bonds, Treasury bills, guaranteed investment contracts (GICs), money market mutual funds and bank accounts, and passbook savings accounts. These are sometimes referred to as *debt instruments* or *fixed-income* investments.

As a lender, you receive a promise that your money will be repaid with interest at a predetermined rate and time. You can calculate your returns with relative certainty, and you expect fewer surprises than with equity or stock investments. If you deposit $1,000 in a one-year CD paying 5 percent interest, you can reasonably anticipate having $1,050 in your account a year later. (This assumes that you will hold onto your debt instrument until it matures.)

With some types of debt investments, though, you are only *promised* that you will be repaid; you are not *guaranteed* repayment of either interest or principal. For example, if you lend your money to a corporation in exchange for a promise to be repaid in five years or 20 years, you run the risk of the corporation going out of business before it repays your loan. Moreover, debt investments are more vulnerable to inflation than stocks. This will be discussed in more detail in the Inflation and Real Rates of Return chapters.

Owning

If you choose to be an owner, you can be an entrepreneur with your money. If you own a business, a piece of real estate, or shares of stock in a corporation, you can benefit from the growth in value of that asset. As an owner, you participate in the fortunes—good and bad—of the asset in which you have invested. If you buy stock in a company selling at $50 per share, you stand to profit if the stock price increases, but you will incur a loss in value if the stock's price declines. Of course, there is no guarantee that any of your money will ever be returned. The company whose stock you own could go bankrupt, making your stock worthless. As we will see in the Volatility chapter, equity investments are subject to uncertainty and unpredictability.

Some stocks also pay dividends, which are distributions of the company's earnings. If 10 million shares of stock are held by investors, and the company decides to distribute $10 million in earnings as dividends, each share of stock will receive a dividend of $1 per share.

NOTE: *Throughout this book "stocks" and "equities" both mean investments in stocks or mutual funds that invest in stocks, or other investments of ownership.*

History of Investment Returns

One surprising thing about the study of historical investment performance is the limited amount of information that was available before 1974. In that year Roger G. Ibbotson and Rex A. Sinquefield published two papers detailing the history of investment returns from 1926 onward.

This landmark work gave investors, analysts and other professionals specific data and information on which to base forecasts of returns for various investments. In fact, with this information the entire world of finance changed. Some of the most comprehensive studies ever done in finance have relied, in part, on the Ibbotson-Sinquefield data.

What Ibbotson and Sinquefield did was to bring the world of investment information into the computer age. The investment community now could track historical returns electronically instead of on paper. Thanks to these two pioneers, we have sophisticated records of historical financial data going back nearly three-quarters of a century for major asset classes such as large- and small-company stocks, long-term government bonds, and Treasury bills. The Ibbotson-Sinquefield study summarizes the historical results of these classes of investments and inflation since the beginning of 1926; it is updated yearly.

This landmark study allows us to examine the historic returns of these asset classes from 1926 to the present and review their characteristics. Such a long-term review may help investors to avoid having unrealistic expectations about future returns. Rates of returns may vary dramatically from month to month, year to year and decade to decade. Examining from 1926 to the present can give both investors and advisors important insights to use in their decision making.

Chart 2-2 tracks the performance of Treasury bills, long-term government bonds, U.S. large-company stocks and U.S. small-company stocks from 1926 through 1996. These are commonly referred to as *asset classes*. Ibbotson-Sinquefield calculated the returns for each entire asset class—not specific stocks, bonds, or Treasury bills within each class. For example, instead of tracking the returns of a single stock such as General Motors, the study measured the average of returns of all large-company stocks in the S&P 500 Index over the 71-year period. The study also tracked inflation, as measured by the Consumer Price Index (CPI), over the same time period.

Chart 2-2
Stocks, Bonds, Bills and Inflation (1926-1996)

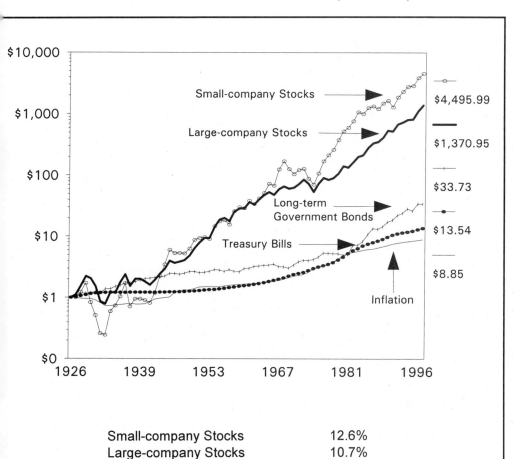

Small-company Stocks	12.6%
Large-company Stocks	10.7%
Long-term Government Bonds	5.1%
Treasury Bills	3.7%
Inflation	3.1%

Ibbotson-Sinquefield calculated how much $1 invested in each of the asset classes would have grown in value from the beginning of 1926 to the present and how inflation diminished the purchasing power of $1. It also translates that performance into average annual compound returns over that time period (these numbers are at the bottom of Chart 2-2). The returns are compound returns; they assume all dividends and interest are reinvested; are calculated before any income taxes have been paid on the growth or income; and do not include any transaction fees, commissions or other costs. Another way of looking at these numbers is to visualize what happens when you invest money in a 401(k), IRA or other tax-deferred investment, where money is accumulated without having to pay current income taxes.

Chart 2-2 does not depict other asset classes such as international stocks and bonds, CDs, corporate bonds, real estate, commodities or precious metals. However, understanding the basic asset classes of investments that are included, and their relationship to inflation, helps you evaluate other investments as well.

Now let's examine the history of inflation and the individual asset classes studied by Ibbotson-Sinquefield for the years 1926 through 1996.

Inflation. The annual compound *inflation* rate over those 71 years has averaged 3.1 percent, meaning the cost of goods and services has increased. A hypothetical basket of groceries for which you would have paid $1 in 1926 would cost $8.85 in 1996; or a lamp that cost $10 in 1926 would sell for $88.50 in 1996.

Chart 2-3
Inflation 1926-1996

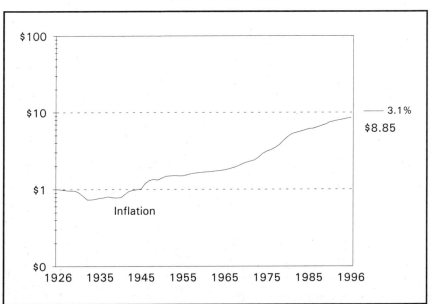

Treasury Bills. *Treasury bills* are short-term loans investors make to the United States government. The period until maturity (when the loan is repaid) can range from a few weeks to one year, and they are sold in increments of $10,000. Treasury bills have the following characteristics: they pay a fixed interest rate with the smallest risk of default of any investment (the U.S. Treasury will always pay its debts because, unlike other borrowers, it owns the printing press); they are very liquid, which means you can get your money on short notice; and they are sold at a discount from their face value and pay no current interest. Thus, if the interest rate is 5 percent on a one-year Treasury bill, an investor would lend the government $9,500 and receive no interest payments during the entire year. At the end of the year, the government would repay the investor $10,000. Treasury bills are considered to be among the safest investments available, and are often described as being "risk-free."

Chart 2-4
Treasury Bills 1926-1996

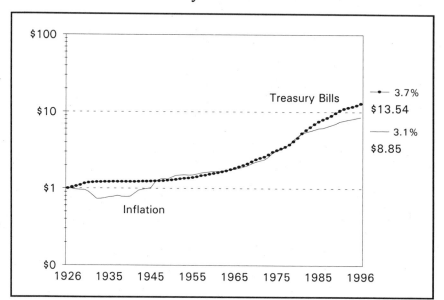

Although there are Treasury bills with different maturities, the Ibbotson-Sinquefield study measures the returns of bills that mature in one month. Thus, these represent short-term cash equivalents, comparable to money market funds and bank savings accounts. Chart 2-4 shows that these investments have posted an average annual compound return of 3.7 percent over the 71-year period. Hence, $1 invested in one-month Treasury bills at the beginning of 1926 and continuously reinvested was worth $13.54 by the end of 1996.

Long-term Government Bonds. *Long-term government bonds* are generally defined as fixed-interest loans to the U.S. government with maturities of greater than 10 years. For this study, Ibbotson-Sinquefield used maturities of 20 years.

Chart 2-5
Long-term Government Bonds 1926-1996

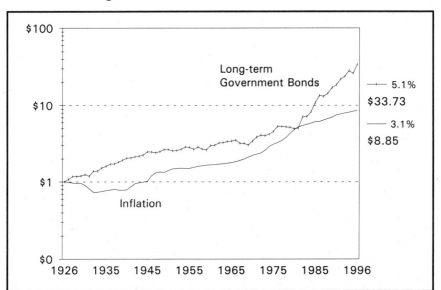

Over this 71 years, 20-year bonds generated an average annual compound return of 5.1 percent, so $1 invested in these bonds at the beginning of 1926 would have grown to $33.73 by the end of 1996. Again, this number assumes that all income generated by the bonds was reinvested each year in more bonds. The long-term returns from Treasury bonds significantly exceeded the returns from Treasury bills. Investors who assumed the interest rate risk associated with longer-term bonds have historically received higher returns.

Long-term U.S. government bonds have two basic characteristics: they have no default risk; but are subject to interest rate risk. Interest rate risk means that if interest rates go up, you will suffer a loss if you sell your bond before its maturity date (since a bond's value falls when interest rates rise). Conversely, if the interest rate goes down after purchase, the bond's value rises and you can have capital appreciation if you sell the bond before its maturity date. The total return on a bond consists of its interest payments plus any price changes due to interest rate fluctuations. Interest income from government bonds is tax-free at the state level.

Suppose you buy a $10,000 20-year Treasury bond that pays 7 percent interest. The government will pay you $700 each year in interest for the next 20 years, and then repay the original $10,000 principal. But if, after a year, the interest rate on the same type of bond rises to 8 percent, a purchaser of a new bond would receive $800 per year in interest for 20 years. Consequently, since your old bond only pays $700 per year, other investors will not pay you $10,000 for it, because they could buy a new bond paying $800 per year for the same price. To sell your bond before its maturity date, you would have to settle for something less than your original $10,000 investment.

On the other hand, if the interest rate on a new 20-year Treasury bond falls to 6 percent during the following year, the value of your old bond goes up. This is because your annual $700 income stream is more valuable to another investor than the government's current offer of $600 per year for a new Treasury bond. So, if you choose to sell your bond before its maturity date, you will receive something more than your original $10,000 investment for it—called "selling at a premium."

We can study Tables 2-2 and 2-3 to estimate how interest rate changes affect the value of existing government bonds with differing lengths of time remaining to maturity. For example, Table 2-2 shows that if the interest rate goes up 2 percent, the value of a bond with 10 years remaining to maturity would go down 13.3 percent. A bond with a face value of $10,000 would thus be sold for $8,770. On the other hand, Table 2-3 shows that, if the interest rate goes down 2 percent, the value of the same bond goes up in value 16 percent. Thus, a buyer might pay you $11,600 should you decide to sell your bond.

The inverse relationship between a bond's market price and the prevailing interest rate can be compared to a teeter-totter, where interest rates sit at one end and the market price of bonds at the other. When one end of the teeter-totter goes up, the other comes down. The degree of the gain or loss in value depends on the number of years until the bond matures, the percentage change in interest rates, and the bond's original interest rate.

Table 2-2
How Much Bond Prices Will Decline
When Interest Rates Increase

Interest Rate Increase	Years to Maturity				
	1 Year	3 Years	7 Years	10 Years	20 Years
0.50%	(0.5%)	(1.3%)	(2.7%)	(3.6%)	(5.3%)
1.00%	(0.9%)	(2.6%)	(5.4%)	(6.9%)	(10.3%)
1.50%	(1.4%)	(3.9%)	(7.9%)	(10.2%)	(14.8%)
2.00%	(1.9%)	(5.2%)	(10.4%)	(13.3%)	(19.1%)
2.50%	(2.3%)	(6.4%)	(12.8%)	(16.3%)	(23.0%)

Note: Table assumes original bond interest rate of 6.5%. Parentheses indicate negative return.

Table 2-3
How Much Bond Prices Will Increase
When Interest Rates Decline

Interest Rate Decline	Years to Maturity				
	1 Year	3 Years	7 Years	10 Years	20 Years
(0.50%)	0.5%	1.4%	2.8%	3.7%	5.8%
(1.00%)	1.0%	2.7%	5.7%	7.6%	12.0%
(1.50%)	1.4%	4.1%	8.8%	11.7%	18.8%
(2.00%)	1.9%	5.6%	11.9%	16.0%	26.2%
(2.50%)	2.4%	7.0%	15.1%	20.4%	34.2%

Note: Table assumes original bond interest rate of 6.5%.

Comparing Individual Bonds and Bond Mutual Funds

Many investors buy bond mutual funds because it enables them to diversify and buy bonds with many different maturity dates. As with any other investment however, such a plan has both advantages and disadvantages. An investor who chooses to own an individual government bond can be sure of receiving the full value of the bond by holding it until the maturity date. There is no such assurance for bond mutual fund investors, because the value of their account depends on the current value of each of the individual bonds held inside the mutual fund, which will fluctuate as interest rates change. There is seldom a single maturity date for a bond mutual fund.

Large-company U.S. Stocks. If you invest in *large-company U.S. stocks,* you become an owner of shares of large corporations—the ones represented by the Standard & Poor's 500 Stock Composite Index (S&P 500). This index tracks 500 of some of the best-known companies on the American stock market, and is determined by the total market value of their outstanding shares. (Prior to March 1957, it consisted of 90 of the largest stocks.)

The market value of these 500 stocks exceeded $7 trillion in 1998. The companies represented in the S&P 500, which include AT&T, Chevron, General Electric, Walt Disney, Coca-Cola and IBM, account for approximately 70 percent of the total value of all stocks publicly traded in the U.S. When you consider that more than 30,000 stocks are publicly traded in the U.S., it is remarkable that these 500 stocks exceeded $7 trillion in 1998.

The S&P 500 stocks are sometimes referred to as "blue-chip" stocks. The companies tend to be leaders in their respective industries and are important within the overall American economy. The S&P 500 companies cover the major economic sectors and about 90 separate industry groups, such as airlines, banking, insurance, broadcast media, aerospace, and defense. Characteristically, many of these companies have paid dividends consistently for many years, and few have ever gone bankrupt.

The market value of a company's stock equals the total number of shares of stock owned by investors, multiplied by the market price of one share. The S&P 500 index is "market weighted": this means that the larger the market value of a stock compared to the value of other stocks in the index, the larger its representation in the overall index. For example, suppose that the S&P 500 was an index of only two stocks. If one stock has a market value of $200 per share and the other stock has a market value of $100 per share, then a person who invested $300 would be investing $200 in the first stock and $100 in the second stock—not $150 in each stock.

This book uses the S&P 500 to represent the performance of large-company stocks. Some investors are more familiar with the Dow Jones Industrial Average, because they hear or read about it in the media. For instance, when news commentators talk about how "the market" performed that day, they generally refer to the Dow Jones Industrial Average, also called "the Dow." The Dow is an average of 30 selected stocks from the New York Stock Exchange; the selected stocks change from time to time. Table 2-4 lists the companies that currently make up the Dow. General Electric is the only company that has been continually included in the Dow since its inception in 1896 (when the Dow consisted of only 12 stocks). These same 30 companies are also included in the S&P 500 Index.

Table 2-4
The 30 Companies of the Dow Jones Industrial Average

Alcoa	Exxon	Minn. Mining & Mfg.
Allied Signal	General Electric	JP Morgan
American Express	General Motors	Phillip Morris
AT&T	Goodyear	Proctor & Gamble
Boeing	Hewlett-Packard	Sears
Caterpillar	IBM	Travelers Group
Chevron	International Paper	Union Carbide
Coca-Cola	Johnson & Johnson	United Technologies
Dupont	McDonald's	Wal-Mart
Eastman Kodak	Merck	Walt Disney

Over the long term, the growth rates of market performance as measured by the Dow and S&P 500 have been remarkably similar. However, the S&P 500 Index is generally used as the benchmark for comparing the investment performance of money managers, mutual funds, and investment advisors.

The stocks in the S&P 500 have earned an average annual compound 10.7 percent return from 1926 through 1996; $1 invested 71 years ago would have grown to $1,371 at the end of 1996. The return from stocks has far exceeded the return from bonds. This historically higher return reflects the greater risks taken by stock investors (or owners) versus those taken by debt investors (or lenders)—a point we will discuss further in the Risk and Volatility chapter.

The returns on most large-company stocks generally come from two sources: the growth in value of the stock, and dividends from the company's earnings. Most large-company stocks pay dividends, although some well known stocks such as United Airlines and Microsoft currently pay no dividends. The total return illustrated in

Chart 2-6 assumes that you continually reinvested dividends to buy additional shares of the same stocks. For the S&P 500 stocks, close to 45 percent of the historic 10.7 percent return was due to the compounding of reinvested dividends, while the balance came from capital growth.

Chart 2-6
Large-company Stocks 1926-1996

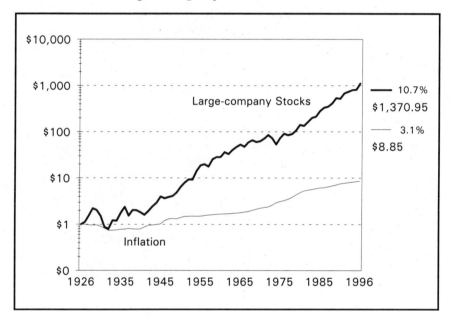

Many investors are surprised to learn that such a high percentage of the total return came from compounded dividends, thinking that almost all of the return was attained through appreciation. Stock investors need to be aware of the role of dividends. Among other things, there are tax implications, since dividends are taxable every year, even if they are reinvested.

Statistical Returns Versus Personal Returns: The Real Story

While historical returns give us valuable insights, they seldom reflect the individual returns investors actually received over the long term. In order to have earned that 10.7 percent return, an investor in large-company stocks would have to purchase the Index on January 1, 1926. He would then sit back for 71 years and not sell those stocks, even during the incredible market fluctuations and stress caused by the Great Depression, World War II, the Korean and Vietnam Wars, political assassinations, the Cold War, the Cuban missile crisis, oil embargoes, and numerous recessions.

And what if during this 71-year period the investor had experienced a divorce, family difficulties, health problems, job loss, depression, loss of a loved one, financial reversals or other personal difficulties? Could he still leave his money invested in these volatile and uncertain stocks? Keeping in mind both statistical history and investors' personal histories leads us to consider the real question: how many investors will actually receive historical returns? In reality, few investors would, which we will explore further later in this chapter.

Small-company U.S. Stocks. The term *small-company stocks* is a bit misleading. The small-company stocks in this asset class may have market valuations of hundreds of millions of dollars, but they are still considered "small" for purposes of the Ibbotson-Sinquefield study. Large-company stocks, by comparison, have market valuations well into the billions of dollars. In Ibbotson-Sinquefield, small-company stocks consist of the smallest 20 percent, by market value, of companies listed on the New York Stock Exchange; and since 1982 they have included certain stocks listed on the American Stock Exchange (AMEX) and other stocks traded over the counter (OTC). Names such as Safeguard Scientific and Allied Products show up on the list, along with household names such as Clorox.

Generally, small-company stocks pay small or no dividends, because they reinvest earnings in company growth and development. Prices of these stocks have historically experienced radical fluctuations.

As measured by Ibbotson-Sinquefield, small-company stocks have returned 12.6 percent average annual compound return; this means that a $1 investment in 1926 would have grown to $4,496 by the end of 1996. Once again, this figure includes no adjustment for taxes or any transaction fees or costs.

Chart 2-7
Small-company U.S. Stocks 1926-1996

Chart 2-7 shows the difference that less than 2 percentage points of compound annual return over a long period of time can make in accumulating wealth. At 10.7 percent, $1 invested in large-company stocks grew to $1,371 in 71 years. But at 12.6 percent (just 1.9 percent more), $1 grew to $4,496 in the same time period invested in small-company stocks. This difference of 1.9 percentage points is just another example of the miracle of compound interest. Differences in rates of return that some investors might consider small (for instance, 1 or 2 percentage points) can produce amazing growth in dollars when compounded over a long period of time.

Upon seeing this extra 1.9 percent return, many investors may want to invest in this asset class. However, before they decide to invest in small-company stocks, they need to understand the incredible market fluctuations they would have had to endure in this asset class. We will explore this in the Risk and Volatility chapter.

Statistical History versus Behavioral History

So far we have discussed historical returns of various asset classes. However, we have not discussed how the behavior of investors can affect investment returns. We may see a mutual fund that advertises an average annual compound return of 15 percent over the past 10 years. But because of their behavior, this advertised return may have no relationship to what individual investors in that fund actually earned.

One of the best ways to separate statistical history from actual returns is to look at a study of mutual fund investors by Dalbar Financial Services, titled "1993 Quantitative Analysis of Investor Behavior." The study tracked money flowing in and out of stock and bond mutual funds from 1984 through 1993 and measured the length of time individual investors remained in the funds, as well as their returns.

During this 10-year period the S&P 500 earned 14 percent average annual compound return. However, the study found that many individual investors in equity mutual funds earned an average of only 4.3 percent compound return during this same period. Why? Investors tended to move in and out of funds, selling after the fund values went down and buying back later after they went up. To quote the study: "Investment return is far more dependent on investor behavior than [on] fund performance." A similar result occurred for investors in bond mutual funds.

Let's look at how an investor's behavior could impact investment returns. Assume that a particular mutual fund's returns over the past five years averaged 25 percent per year. An investor buys the fund expecting similar returns, but the fund subsequently performs substantially below its 5-year track record. The investor becomes impatient and disenchanted, sells the fund and chooses another investment looking for those higher returns. Statistics are usually based on a "buy and hold" strategy, but investors often have difficulty holding on, particularily in a prolonged down market.

The results of the Dalbar study and other research reinforce the importance of personal behavior as an influence on investment performance and provide an excellent reminder that investors must not only focus on statistical history. Only by understanding behavior can investors be equipped to meet the enormous challenge of both thinking and acting for the long term with their investments. However, if investors have not personally experienced a prolonged down market or have only had generally favorable investment experiences, it may be easy to dismiss the powerful influence of behavior on long-term investment performance.

Investment History—Do We Want to Rely on it?

We've looked at 71 years of investment history, and seen that stocks have produced significantly higher returns over the long term than government bonds and Treasury bills. However, when making investment decisions all investors and advisors must consider the following two questions:

- Do I think investment history will repeat itself?

- Should I rely on investment history when making my investment decisions?

Experts have long debated whether investment history will repeat itself. Of the arguments that it will, perhaps the most persuasive is based on an understanding of human nature. As humans we prefer certainty to uncertainty, predictability to unpredictability and the familiar to the unfamiliar, particularly when it comes to money.

In the Risk and Volatility chapter we will see that stocks are more volatile than bonds and bonds more volatile than risk-free investments. As long as human nature does not change, as long as people prefer certainty and predictability with their investments, maybe the best rationale for assuming that investment history will repeat itself is the notion that people need to be rewarded for incurring additional risk. And the close connection between risk and return will remain.

Uncertainty and Unpredictability

When we choose to invest in stocks we volunteer to enter a world of uncertainty and unpredictability. To better understand this, it may help to look first at the social, political, and economic world we live in. Let's consider a few examples of the uncertainty around us.

For nearly 50 years, America and its allies fought the Cold War; then, almost overnight, the Soviet Union broke up and the Berlin Wall came down. When a bomb unexpectedly exploded in 1993 in New York City's World Trade Center, it brought foreign terrorism to the United States for the first time. In the 1960s, experts predicted that we were headed for a significantly shorter work week and that we would have a problem adjusting to the additional leisure time. Instead, the work week has actually increased by a staggering 13 hours for the average worker. In 1973 an unlimited oil supply was taken for granted. But the OPEC oil embargo caused the price of gasoline to rocket from 30 cents per gallon to over a dollar, gasoline was rationed, and long lines appeared at every local gas station. All of these events were considered unthinkable before they occurred.

For many years, the world's largest corporation was General Motors. In 1985 it employed over 500,000 people in the United States alone. But by the end of 1996 the total G.M. work force in the U.S. was 300,000. Numerous other major U.S. corporations followed suit and drastically reduced their work forces. For the first time ever in its corporate history, IBM announced job layoffs.

Stocks and the stock market cannot escape their own uncertainty and unpredictability. The makers of Tylenol, one of the leading pain relievers, suddenly found their product's reputation damaged when someone injected poison into random packages. This tampering led to the recall of several million packages of Tylenol and a sharp drop in sales. Earnings for the parent company, Johnson & Johnson, fell significantly and the stock price plummeted. For years, Dow Corning was a prosperous company, growing to more than $2 billion in annual sales. However, faced with a mass of lawsuits related to its silicone breast implants, the company filed for bankruptcy.

Imagine yourself investing in the Nikkei Index, the standard for measuring the value of large-company Japanese stocks. The Nikkei Index includes major corporations such as Sony, Toyota, NEC, and Mitsubishi, companies that the rest of the world was attempting to emulate because of their unique capabilities in management, manufacturing and inventory techniques. At the start of 1990 the Nikkei Index was close to 40,000, but by the end of the year it had plummeted to 22,400. Worse yet, eight long years later, the index had still not recovered and was hovering around 14,000 in 1998.

Investors, from 1990 to 1998, lost over 60% of their value; imagine being invested for this long and have your assets be worth only 40 cents on the dollar. And this from a country that was a model for economic growth and stability.

Market declines have not been limited to Japan in the 1990s. Emerging markets, such as Mexico, Malaysia, most of Latin America, Thailand, Indonesia, and Korea all suffered significant market losses and ongoing economic chaos. Most of these market declines were even steeper than Japan's.

These are just a few of the countless examples that show why investing in the stock market means subjecting your money to an unpredictable and uncertain world.

Stocks: Volunteering for Combat

Another way to appreciate the historical relationship between risk and return is to imagine yourself in the military. Your commanding officer is looking for volunteers for a hazardous assignment that may include going into combat. If you volunteer, you will receive hazardous-duty pay. You will be rewarded for taking the extra risk that others do not, because you will be subjecting yourself to potential injury or death.

Similarly, if you buy individual stocks or invest in a mutual fund that owns stocks, you are volunteering to go into combat, entering an investment world of unpredictability and uncertainty. Like the soldier, you are potentially placing yourself in harm's way. You hope to be rewarded for this risk in the form of higher returns. However, it is essential to understand that a soldier is *guaranteed* extra pay for taking risk. When an investor volunteers for higher risk by investing in more volatile asset classes such as stocks, hazardous duty pay may be *expected*, but it is *not guaranteed*. The terrible truth is, despite the compelling evidence that higher long-term risks have been rewarded with higher returns historically, it's always possible that your money could be worth less in the future, regardless of the length of the investment war.

If you believe that investment history will repeat itself you may be inclined to invest in stocks because historically they have outper-formed bonds and other forms of lending. But proper investment decisions are not so simple, due to various types of history, other dimensions of risk and volatility, and numerous personal factors that must be considered, which we will discuss in future chapters.

Summary: Tools for the Savvy Investor

A firm grounding in investment history and fundamentals can help you in various ways.

- The landmark research of the Ibbotson-Sinquefield study gives you information on long-term investment performance of various asset classes and shows how they performed in relationship to each other. This historical information provides a frame of reference for expected long-term returns on your investments.

- You can see that how you design your portfolio—your investment allocation among various asset classes—is an important factor in determining your portfolio's long-term investment performance.

- Even though there is an endless number of investment choices, they boil down to two basic ways of investing money: you can be a lender or an owner. Understanding the differences will assist you to have realistic expectations.

- Answering the question, "will I rely on investment history to repeat itself?" can assist you to make critical choices about selecting investments and advisors, and in your ability to remain committed to a long-term investment policy.

- You can see that historical investment returns do not tell the whole story. You must also consider what investors had to endure to get those returns—including market fluctuations, social and political events and personal difficulties.

- Your investment performance may be affected more by your personal behavior than by the market's behavior. Understanding this may encourage you not to let your emotions influence your investment decisions.

INFLATION: THE SILENT KILLER

Some Terrible Truths

- Inflation is the silent killer of an investor's purchasing power.

- Investors will have to accumulate 50 to 100 percent more money just to pay for inflation after they retire.

- Investors can believe they are earning positive returns when, in fact, they are not.

- IRAs, 401(k)s, and profit sharing plans have no inflation protection.

- Regardless of the government's stated inflation rate, inflation remains a terrible threat.

Inflation's Threat

Inflation poses a great threat to many people's long-term financial security and their ability to retire. But unlike mutual funds or stock and bond prices, inflation's daily fluctuations are not tracked in the newspaper. Inflation is an invisible, silent killer—the high blood pressure of the financial world. Just as you can have high blood pressure for years and not know it until you suffer from its consequences, inflation can quietly shrink the purchasing power of your dollars without you even realizing you are at risk.

Simply stated, inflation erodes your money's value. It makes the same products or services you buy today cost more in the future, whether you buy a haircut, a house or a loaf of bread. Although it may be easy to understand what inflation is, it is often difficult to grasp what it will do to you. Inflation can cause today's goods and services to more than double or triple in price by the time you retire, and may cost nearly 10 times or more in your later retirement years.

It is easy to take inflation too lightly because it seems so benign. When you hear that the inflation rate for a particular year was 3 percent, you might think, "That's three cents on the dollar, what's the big deal?" However, the impact of a few pennies compounded over a number of years can significantly undermine your chances of achieving your investment and retirement goals. Just ask those who have already retired and seen the purchasing power of their fixed income slowly erode over 10, 20 or 30 years.

In This Chapter...

We will look at the impact of inflation both on the cost of everyday items and on the amount of capital you may need in the future to pay for retirement. By examining some familiar charts that demonstrate how inflation affects your future purchasing power, and looking at the same numbers in a different way, you may gain better insight into what we call "the silent killer." By converting these charts to dollars, we will demonstrate how devastating inflation really is.

We will review what makes up the government's Consumer Price Index. Just as important, we will look at what factors are not being considered, which tend to underestimate our true cost of living. We will also look at inflation during different historical time periods.

Further, we will look at why people will have to deal with inflation for longer periods than ever before. We will then discuss a major issue many investors will have to confront—the sobering fact that 401(k) plans and IRAs provide no cost of living increases. Finally, we will see how investors who perceive that they have favorable investment returns actually lose ground after taxes and inflation.

Inflated Purchase Prices

We have all seen evidence of inflation. A new full-sized Chevrolet cost $2,500 35 years ago; a comparable vehicle costs in excess of $25,000 today—more than my parents paid for their first house. Years ago you could have had a campus building named after you for donating the same amount that a four-year education now costs at many private colleges. Table 3-1 lists some other consumer items whose prices have changed over time. These prices did not skyrocket overnight; they grew gradually over a long period. They *inflated*.

Table 3-1
Changes in Prices Between 1962 and 1997

Item	Average 1962 Price	Average 1997 Price	Percentage Increase
Hershey bar	$ .05	$ .65	1,300%
New York Times	.05	1.00	2,000%
First-class postage	.04	.32	800%
Gasoline (gallon)	.31	1.35	440%
Hamburger (Big Mac)	.28	1.59	570%
CPI	1.00	5.05	488%

Inflation also affects us in many less obvious ways than in the growing sticker prices of automobiles and other consumer items. Higher tax rates are a hidden form of inflation. For example, the maximum amount of Social Security (FICA) taxes deducted from a paycheck was $30 per year in the early 1950s. In 1998, the maximum was $5,233 a year—an increase of more than 15,000 percent.

Someone once asked me if there was anything positive about inflation. After thinking about it for awhile I answered, "Well, a kid can't get sick on a nickel's worth of candy anymore."

Inflation During Retirement

Any investor who is not convinced about the debilitating impact of inflation should talk to someone who has been retired for a number of years. Retirees who no longer receive a regular paycheck truly see what happens when the cost of goods and services increase. When the subject of inflation comes up, they generally respond: "You bet I understand inflation! You should see how much it costs me to live today compared with just ten years ago."

History of Inflation

Statistics on inflation are tracked by the Consumer Price Index (CPI), which is made up of an average of retail prices for a basket of consumer goods and services, as calculated by the U.S. Department of Labor. Currently, the basket contains 184 items, ranging from ground beef to college tuition. Items are categorized into seven broad groups: food and beverages; housing; apparel; medical care; transportation; entertainment; and other goods and services. The annual changes in price of these items are stated as a percentage, which is termed the *cost-of-living adjustment*. Over the years the government has changed its method of calculating the CPI a number of times.

There is much discussion today about another change or modification in how the current CPI is calculated. But merely lowering the CPI is not going to affect us as consumers when we go into stores or car dealerships, pay for health care costs or insurance, or pay for our childrens' education.

When the prices of the goods included in the index are collectively higher, we have inflation. But the collective prices have not always increased. When prices decline, we have *deflation*. That phenomenon existed in the early 1930s; from 1926 to the present, deflation has occurred 9 times.

From 1992 through 1996, the annual inflation rate averaged less than 3.0 percent. However, for the 25-year period from 1972 through 1996, the average inflation rate was a staggering 5.6 percent, a surprise to many investors. And going back to the end of World War II in 1945, the over-50-year average rate of inflation exceeded 4 percent annually.

Personal Inflation Rates

It is important to note that the national CPI numbers may be significantly higher or lower than what your own *personal inflation rate* may be. Inflation increases could be different for each person or family, based on the goods and services they purchase to support their particular lifestyle. The cost of housing, food, taxes, services, clothes and other items also vary in different cities and regions across this country.

Even though inflation during the 1990s has been lower than what we have experienced over the past 25 years, it is dangerous to rely on a short-term period as a basis for making long-term decisions. Data for short-term periods seldom reflect what happens over the long term, whether it be inflation or investment returns. Trouble is, human nature leads us to believe that our short-term experiences over the recent past will represent what we will experience permanently over the long term. Because the 1990s have produced an average inflation rate of around 3 percent, many individuals today will predict a future inflation rate of around 3 percent. Similarly, in the late 1970s and early 1980s, when the Consumer Price Index was over 10 percent, many predicted that future inflation would average 8 percent or higher.

In this chapter, we assume an inflation rate of 3.5 percent. Some may feel comfortable using lower inflation rates, say 2 or 3 percent, and others will use higher rates. But differing inflation rates over the long term will not alter the enormous challenge that inflation poses to investors.

NOTE: *If an individual assumes that inflation will be low over the long term, or that we will experience deflation, experts would anticipate that the long-term returns of both stocks and bonds would adjust downward as well. See chapter on Real Rates of Return.*

The Loss of Purchasing Power Over Time

An excellent exercise to remind us of how inflation impacts purchasing power is to look at the following chart that tracks a single block of money over a number of years. Chart 3-1 demonstrates how inflation erodes our purchasing power over time. We'll see how much $10,000 in today's money will purchase in the future if inflation averages a hypothetical 3.5 percent, which is less than the 50-year historical average since World War II.

Chart 3-1
The Loss of Purchasing Power Over Time
(3.5% Annual Inflation)

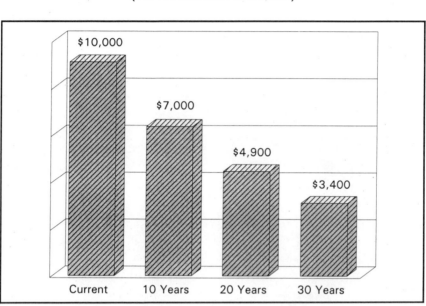

The first bar in Chart 3-1 shows the $10,000 that you are using today to buy goods and services such as food, clothing and utilities. The next bar, representing the value of your money 10 years later, indicates that your $10,000 will buy only $7,000 of the same goods and services. The third bar shows that 20 years from now, today's $10,000 will buy only $4,900 worth of the same goods and services. Another way of looking at lost purchasing power is to think of going to the supermarket in the future. You give the clerk $1 for a loaf of bread, but the clerk says, "Sorry, we don't sell bread by the slice!" That's what inflation does to your spending power.

The last bar in Chart 3-1 shows that, in 30 years, today's $10,000 will buy goods and services worth only $3,400 today. That is a 65 percent reduction in purchasing power. If investors do not factor inflation into their long-term plans, they may not be able to achieve educational or other important goals, and may subject themselves to a significantly lower standard of living. In addition, they could run out of money in retirement or find themselves dependent on family or government.

Inflation and the Two-income Family

All of us have seen many changes in the American family and workplace, including a dramatic increase in the number of two-income families and the number of individuals who are working significantly longer hours just to maintain their standard of living. Many families need those two incomes, or work longer hours, because of the 5.6 percent inflation rate over the past 25 years and the dramatic increase in Social Security taxes. Today, we need almost four dollars for every dollar we spent 25 years ago—*a staggering 400 percent increase.*

Maintaining Purchasing Power

To avoid losing the purchasing power of your dollars and to maintain your current standard of living in the future, how much money do you need? Chart 3-2 takes the same $10,000 we tracked in Chart 3-1 and the same 3.5 percent average inflation rate, and shows how much it will cost in future dollars to buy the same goods and services we use today.

Chart 3-2
Impact of 3.5% Annual Inflation on $10,000 Over Time

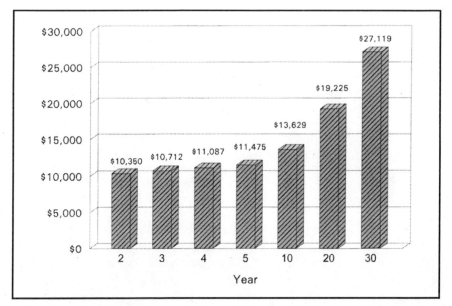

The goods and services that cost $10,000 this year will cost $10,350 the following year. Although this increase may not seem dramatic, we can see that the year-to-year changes keep adding up. In just 10 years you will need $13,629 to buy $10,000 worth of goods and services. You have not moved to a different neighborhood; you are shopping at the same store; you have not raised your standard of living. The increased cost is incurred simply to *maintain* your original standard of living.

Incredibly, in 20 years, you will need more than $19,000 to pay for each group of goods and services that now cost $10,000. Imagine that you are on your way to buy a new car priced at $20,000, but you fall asleep for 20 years like Rip Van Winkle. When you wake up, you walk into a car dealership ready to buy that new car, but now the price tag is $48,000. Most readers can recall the price of something from their own experience 15 or 20 years ago—perhaps the cost of a movie ticket, an ice cream cone or a haircut—whose price has increased similarly.

Many people looking at Chart 3-2 find it hard to comprehend that 15 or 20 years in the future, even with modest inflation, they could be spending double what they do now. Numerous charts demonstrate the "magic of compound interest" by showing how dramatically a single contribution to an IRA or 401(k) plan can grow over a person's working years. Unfortunately, the flip side of this is "the tragedy of compounding inflation." The terrible truth is that most investors will need the magic to avert the tragedy.

Inflation Assumptions in Financial Modeling

An increasing number of investors and advisors use computer software to calculate projections for their retirement planning and investment decision making. Critical attention must be paid to the assumptions used in software for future inflation rates. In these projections, even a small difference in the assumptions, just one percent for example, can mean needing to accumulate hundreds of thousands of dollars more to retire or having to work years beyond an expected retirement age. One might look at this as sending a rocket to the moon. Mission Control says the good news is your trajectory is off by only one percent; the bad news is you eventually will land on Neptune.

A Different Look at Inflation

You may have seen charts similar to Charts 3-1 and 3-2 in newspapers, magazines, 401(k) presentations or books discussing inflation. They all show the loss of purchasing power or the increase in cost of living over time. You may understand the information intellectually, but these types of charts and statistics do not provide a full and complete picture of the situation. It may be interesting to know how little today's dollar will buy in the future or how many dollars must be spent in the future to buy the same goods and services as today. For planning purposes, however, you need to know how many dollars you must accumulate in order to protect your lifestyle from future inflation.

Because retirement needs are the single biggest reason that people invest, a good way to understand the havoc inflation can wreak is to determine how much you will have to accumulate by retirement day in order to provide a certain income stream through-out your retirement years. We will work with the same $10,000 block of money as in the previous examples, in order to capture the impact of inflation in a different way.

For this illustration, assume that a couple wants to know how much capital they need to amass to provide an annual income of $10,000 for 25 years. If we assume a 7.5 percent rate of return, and if we assume that principal and interest are to be totally depleted at the end of 25 years, we would find that the couple must accumulate $110,000. However, the couple also wants their income to keep up with 3.5 percent inflation, so they can purchase the same quantity and quality of goods and services every year. To do this, they must accumulate more than $153,000—a sobering 40 percent increase over the amount needed in the absence of inflation, just to pay for the seemingly small, incremental cost-of-living increases that occur year after year. Chart 3-3 illustrates this example.

If the couple wanted to provide $40,000 a year (inflation-ad-justed) they would have to accumulate four times as much, or $612,000. These calculations do not include income taxes, which will substantially increase the amount of money the couple would need.

Chart 3-3
The Impact of Inflation on a Lump-Sum Amount

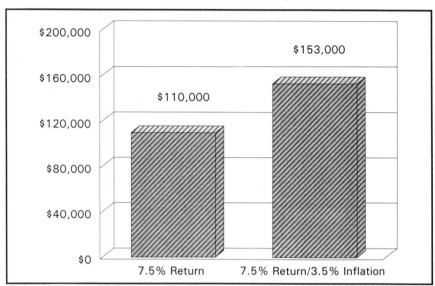

Protecting Your Retirement Years from Inflation

In our previous example, we looked at providing an inflation-adjusted income for 25 years of retirement. For many people, retirement will be even longer, perhaps 30 years or more. Why? For one thing, more and more individuals are taking early retirement. For another, the average joint life expectancy for a couple today is approximately age 90.

There is another factor that we must consider. Many people will face major changes occurring in the work force, not only today but also in the future. Many large companies are downsizing for economic reasons. In addition, technology is changing at such a rapid pace that many jobs today will either become obsolete or employees may not be able to keep up with the pace. Longer-term job security has become the exception and not the norm. As a result, many investors will have far longer periods of time in retirement than they anticipated due to their *involuntary* early retirement.

Chart 3-4 uses the same assumptions as Chart 3-3 (7.5 percent rate of return and 3.5 percent inflation, a $10,000 annual income stream) and shows the amount of money needed to provide for 25, 30, 35, and 40 years of retirement. Again, taxes have not been factored into these lump sums, which for most investors will significantly increase the amounts needed. This will be discussed further in the Real Rates of Return chapter.

Chart 3-4
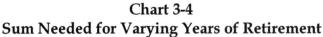
Sum Needed for Varying Years of Retirement

Realistic Assumptions?

So far in this chapter, we have used a 7.5 percent rate of return and a 3.5 percent rate of inflation. Some readers will say the rate of return is too low; others may feel that the inflation rate is too high. Yet whatever the inflation rate or the investment rate of return, the challenge that inflation poses to today's investor will not go away.

Inflation and Defined Benefit Plans

Many individuals, particularly those who have worked for large employers or for government, participate in defined benefit pension plans, which generally provide a monthly income for life after the employee retires. But while receiving a monthly check for life offers great security, many such plans do not offer a cost-of-living adjustment (COLA) or, if they do, impose significant limitations on COLAs now or in the future. Persons fortunate enough to be covered by such plans must still plan for, *and pay for*, inflation when the purchasing power of their pension checks gradually dwindles.

For example, suppose that an employee who expects to live 25 years in retirement receives $10,000 a year from a pension plan that includes no cost-of-living adjustment. Clearly, the purchasing power of the $10,000 payments will erode year by year due to inflation, since the pension amount will remain the same. As illustrated in Chart 3-3, a retiree needs an extra $43,000 just to keep up with inflation on that $10,000 of annual income. Others might need even more money, if they have a longer retirement, a lower portfolio return, or a higher personal rate of inflation.

Thus, employees who do not get a full cost-of-living adjustment from their defined benefit pension plans will have to pick up the tab for inflation from their personal savings—a tab that could be enormous! Many employees will find they have to accumulate hundreds of thousands of dollars to protect their standard of living after retirement, over and above their pension plan income.

IRAs, 401(k)s and Profit Sharing Plans and the Cost of Living

The trend today is away from defined benefit pension plans and toward tax-deferred retirement plans such as 401(k)s, IRAs and profit sharing plans. It is essential for investors to remember that moneys invested in such plans do not have any cost of living increases. Thus, investors in these plans have three burdens they must carry. They are responsible for accumulating enough money to provide the needed income stream in retirement; they are responsible for making investment decisions on how to invest their retirement savings; and what is generally not discussed, they are responsible for picking up the enormous tab for inflation. *These three onerous burdens forced upon the American investor are unprecedented in history.*

Returns After Inflation and Taxes

We have discussed how inflation quietly erodes our purchasing dollars over a long period of time. However, when we add taxes in combination with inflation the overall impact is even more devastating. Taxes and inflation can affect all investors, but it can be particularly hard on investors who lend their personal taxable money through bonds, Treasury bills, or certificates of deposit (CDs). Let's examine the net returns of investors in one-year CDs.

Table 3-2 illustrates the rate of return after taxes and inflation that an investor would have received on CDs for each year from 1972 through 1997. To keep the example simple, we used a hypothetical average tax rate of 25 percent. Of course, an investor's actual tax bill depends on income, deductions, the existence of a state income tax, and other factors.

For each year listed in the table, you see the rate a CD earned during that year, the deduction for taxes, the net return after taxes, the inflation rate, and then the rate of return after taxes and inflation. In 1974, for example, CDs paid investors 11.0 percent interest. With an income tax rate of 25 percent, 2.8 percent of the 11 percent interest would be paid to the government, leaving investors with a 8.2 percent return. But inflation that year was 12.2 percent, so the return for investors after taxes and inflation was actually *negative* 4.0 percent.

Let's take this result and convert it into dollars. If you had $1,000 invested in a CD in 1974, your $1,000 would be worth $1,110 at the end of the year. Then the government taxed you 25 percent on your investment earnings, reducing your account to $1,082. Unfortunately, inflation was 12.2 percent, which reduced your purchasing power to $950. So, in reality, you lost money, despite the fact that the CD carried a hefty 11 percent interest rate.

The shaded rows in Table 3-2 show that close to 40 percent of the time between 1972 and 1997 (10 out of 26 years), CD investors experienced a reduction in purchasing power after subtracting taxes and inflation from their returns.

Table 3-2
CD Return After Inflation an
(Expressed in Percentages) 19

Year	CD Rate	Taxes @ 25 %	After-tax Return		
1972	4.5	1.1	3.4	3.4	0.0
1973	8.5	2.1	6.4	8.8	(2.4)
1974	11.0	2.8	8.2	12.2	(4.0)
1975	6.6	1.7	4.9	7.0	(2.1)
1976	5.3	1.3	4.0	4.8	(0.8)
1977	5.5	1.4	4.1	6.8	(2.7)
1978	8.1	2.0	6.1	9.0	(2.9)
1979	11.4	2.9	8.6	13.3	(4.7)
1980	13.6	3.4	10.2	12.4	(2.2)
1981	17.3	4.3	13.0	8.9	4.1
1982	13.0	3.3	9.7	3.9	5.8
1983	9.4	2.4	7.0	3.8	3.2
1984	10.9	2.7	8.2	4.0	4.2
1985	8.3	2.1	6.2	3.8	2.4
1986	6.9	1.7	5.2	1.1	4.1
1987	6.6	1.7	4.9	4.4	0.5
1988	7.3	1.8	5.5	4.4	1.1
1989	9.2	2.3	6.9	4.6	2.3
1990	8.2	2.1	6.1	6.1	0.0
1991	6.0	1.5	4.5	3.1	1.4
1992	3.4	0.9	2.6	3.0	(0.4)
1993	2.7	0.7	2.0	2.8	(0.8)
1994	3.7	0.9	2.8	2.7	0.1
1995	5.4	1.4	4.0	2.7	1.3
1996	4.9	1.2	3.7	3.3	0.4
1997	5.4	1.4	4.0	2.1	1.9

Note: Parentheses indicate negative return.

ata for this 26-year period supply a statistical history of what curred for CD investors, but it does not show how investors reacted emotionally to their returns. For example, in 1974 an investor may have been delighted with the 11.0 percent return on a CD. But Table 3-2 reveals that investor experienced a negative 4.0 percent change in purchasing power after taxes and inflation, from $1,000 (the face value of the CD at the beginning of the year) to $950 at the end of the year. However, the same investor may have been disappointed in 1986 with a 6.9 percent return on a $1,000 CD, even though at the end of the year it produced an increase in purchasing power of $41 to $1,041 after inflation and taxes.

Summary: Tools for the Savvy Investor

What can you gain by coming to grips with inflation, the silent killer? You can apply your understanding of the enormous risk that inflation poses in a number of ways:

- You understand the threat that inflation poses to achieving your retirement and other personal financial goals.

- You will be wary when using short-term inflation rates for long-term planning, since short-term experiences generally have been a poor indicator of actual longer-term results.

- By first determining the capital necessary to create an income stream, and then adding even a moderate inflation rate, you can more accurately project the enormous amount of capital necessary to pay for retirement.

- If you participate in a 401(k), IRA or other tax-deferred retirement plan, recognize that you are responsible for not only accumulating enough money to provide your desired income stream in retirement but also that you must accumulate enough additional assets to pay for inflation.

- You now understand how investors can receive what appears to be an attractive return, but in fact may actually lose real purchasing dollars after inflation and taxes.

REAL RATES OF RETURN: THE RELIABLE YARDSTICK

Some Terrible Truths

- Investors focus on their investment's performance, not on their real rates of return.

- Investors significantly underestimate the amount of money needed for retirement.

- Both "conservative" and "aggressive" investment portfolios in retirement can be far riskier than many investors think.

- Without using real rates of return it may be impossible to determine how much you will need to retire.

- Not enough attention is paid to taxes in retirement planning and investing.

When people think or talk about investing, the first thing that comes to mind is the return they are getting on their investments. Newspaper advertisements and magazine articles list current top-performing mutual funds. Reports from investment advisors, brokerage firms, mutual funds, and 401(k) plans show the returns on investment accounts. Financial publications emphasize stories of companies whose stocks have soared or plunged in value, or of advisors who exceeded the average returns of the market during the past month, quarter, year or decade. Returns are what people see, talk about, and use to measure performance. They are the numbers that provoke investors' emotions. Declining returns make people concerned, anxious, and fearful; rising returns make them feel confident, happy and excited.

The returns you get on your investments are obviously important. However, it is even more important to understand your expected rate of return in relation to inflation, which is your *real rate of return*. A simple definition of real rate of return is the actual return minus the rate of inflation. For example, if an investment earns 8 percent and the rate of inflation is 3 percent, the real rate of return is 5 percent.

Without understanding real rates of return, investors will be hard pressed to estimate how many dollars they will need to retire. Such an understanding is also essential for making difficult decisions about which investments to select and which type of risk to undertake with your investments.

We rarely hear discussions about real rates of return, even though they are the single most influential factor in attaining long-term financial goals. In the Inflation chapter we saw how inflation erodes the purchasing power of money set aside to pay for goods and services in the future. Failing to attain a high enough rate of return over inflation on your investments may leave you with too little money to pay for your children's education. It may force you to significantly reduce your future standard of living. You may not be able to retire when you wish, or you could run out of money during your retirement.

In This Chapter...

We will first look at charts that identify the amount of money necessary to produce an inflation-adjusted income stream. This will clearly demonstrate the importance of real rates of return to you. We will also revisit the history of the returns of various asset classes from 1926 through 1996. This time we will look not only at the returns of the asset classes, but examine them in relationship to inflation in order to see what their real rates of return were.

We then will look at the real rates of return of the same asset classes over a recent 25-year period (from 1972 through 1996)—a period that contained high inflation, low inflation, prolonged up markets and prolonged down markets. Reviewing a history of returns in relation to inflation can provide you with enormous insights for making future investment decisions, as well as help you avoid unrealistic assumptions when using computer programs or worksheets for retirement planning. It can also help you evaluate your portfolio's potential to earn the real return necessary to attain essential financial goals.

The examination of historical real rates of return will allow you to benefit from a table designed to more realistically estimate the assets you need to pay for retirement. After reviewing this table, many investors will realize that their needs for retirement are significantly greater than they had thought.

Finally, we will examine the enormous impact income taxes have on the lump sums needed for retirement, with an emphasis on money coming from IRAs, 401(k)s and other retirement plans.

The Importance of Real Rates of Return

A good way to demonstrate why your real rate of return is so critical is to use an example from the Inflation chapter. Remember the couple who needed to accumulate $153,000 in order to provide an inflation-adjusted $10,000 income stream each year for 25 years? (See Chart 4-1.) We assumed their investment return was 7.5 percent, and inflation was 3.5 percent, so their real rate of return was 4 percent.

Chart 4-1
The Impact of Inflation on Lump-sum Amount

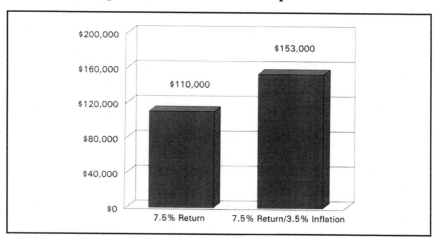

However, what would happen if the same couple were to earn higher or lower investment returns and experience higher or lower inflation rates over this 25-year period, but their real rate of return remained at 4 percent? Under these conditions the lump sum needed to provide the desired annual income stream *would remain virtually the same*. Table 4-1 compares how various rates of return and inflation affect the lump sum that our hypothetical couple needs to accumulate in order to provide $10,000 of annual inflation-adjusted pre-tax income during retirement.

Table 4-1
Assets Required with Various Rates of Return and Inflation
Real Rate of Return: 4%

Income Flow: Inflation-Adjusted $10,000 per year for 25 Years					
Investment Return	10.5%	9.5%	8.5%	7.5%	6.5%
Minus Inflation	6.5%	5.5%	4.5%	3.5%	2.5%
Real Rate of Return	4.0%	4.0%	4.0%	4.0%	4.0%
Lump Sum Needed	$150,500	$151,000	$152,000	$153,000	$154,000

Note: Numbers rounded

The shaded column in Table 4-1 recaps our earlier example where a couple earning a 7.5 percent return with 3.5 percent inflation rate netted a 4 percent real rate of return and needed $153,000 to provide a $10,000 inflation-adjusted income stream for 25 years. Now let's examine what would happen if the couple earned a 6.5 percent return but the inflation rate was 2.5 percent—again resulting in a 4 percent real rate of return. How many dollars would the couple need with this combination of a lower investment return and a lower inflation rate? They need $154,000—just $1,000 more.

What if both the investment return and the inflation rate were higher? If the investment return was 9.5 percent with a 5.5 percent inflation rate, you might expect this higher return to significantly alter the lump sum needed. But Table 4-1 illustrates the dollars needed are approximately the same: $151,000. Remember, the real rate of return is once again 4 percent, and the amounts do not factor in income taxes.

As we can see from the table, *if the real rate of return (the investment return minus inflation) doesn't change, the lump sum necessary to achieve an important financial goal remains essentially the same regardless of investment returns or inflation rates.* If the real rate of return remains constant at 4 percent, the lump sum needed by the couple remains remarkably stable to provide the hypothetical inflation-adjusted income stream for 25 years.

Let's review this important concept again, but let's suppose that this time the couple wants to know what impact a 6 percent real rate of return would have on the lump sum they need for retirement.

Table 4-2
Assets Required with Various Rates of Return and Inflation
Real Rate of Return: 6%

Income Flow: Inflation-Adjusted $10,000 per Year for 25 Years				
Investment Return	11.5%	10.5%	9.5%	8.5%	7.5%
Minus Inflation	5.5%	4.5%	3.5%	2.5%	1.5%
Real Rate of Return	6.0%	6.0%	6.0%	6.0%	6.0%
Lump Sum Needed	$125,000	$125,000	$126,000	$126,500	$127,000

Note: Numbers rounded

The first thing you'll notice in Table 4-2 is that the lump sum needed has decreased substantially—from around $150,000 to approximately $125,000. This is because the real rate of return is now 6 percent, a 50 percent increase over the previously illustrated 4 percent real rate of return.

Again we see that, regardless of investment returns and inflation rates, if the real rate of return remains the same, the lump sum necessary to achieve an important financial goal such as retirement will not substantially change. However, as we will see when we examine historical real rates of return, earning an additional 2 percent real rate of return over the long term can be difficult and may have far-reaching implications when it comes to choosing what type of investments to include in an investment portfolio.

Investors must think about what the portfolio's expected rate of return over inflation will be and not simply focus on investment returns. Only the real rate of return can tell us how much money must be accumulated to provide inflation-adjusted income in the future. Achieving a high investment return might give investors something to talk about. But their investments' long-term *real rate of return* is information investors can truly *use*.

A History of Real Rates of Return

In our previous examples we looked at hypothetical real rates of return. Now let's turn to the history of Treasury bills, long-term government bonds, and large- and small-company U.S. stocks to see the real rates of return for these asset classes from 1926 through 1996 using the data we reviewed in the chapter on Investment History and Fundamentals.

Table 4-3
Compound Rates of Return for Different Asset Classes,
in Relation to Inflation, 1926-1996

Treasury Bills	3.7%
Inflation	-3.1%
Real Rate of Return	0.6%
Long-term Government bonds	5.1%
Inflation	-3.1%
Real Rate of Return	2.0%
Large-company Stocks (S&P 500)	10.7%
Inflation	-3.1%
Real Rate of Return	7.6%
Small-company Stocks	12.6%
Inflation	-3.1%
Real Rate of Return	9.5%

When the historical rate of inflation is subtracted from the historical compound rate of return for each of these four asset classes, as demonstrated in Table 4-3, the real rate of return for each class is revealed. For example, from 1926 through 1996 Treasury bill investors saw their portfolios grow by an average annual compound return of 3.7 percent per year. Because the inflation rate during this period was 3.1 percent, however, the true purchasing power of their portfolios grew by an average of only six-tenths of 1 percent (0.6) per year. In contrast, investors in stocks of the S&P 500 enjoyed a compound rate of return of 10.7 percent; because inflation was 3.1 percent, their real rate of return was 7.6 percent.

Historical Returns Are Easily Overestimated

It is important for investors to realize that the average annual compound returns as shown in Tables 4-3 and 4-4 for all asset classes include the reinvestment of all dividends and interest during the entire period. The returns do not take into consideration any commissions, transaction costs, administration fees, or any other form of expenses that are a normal part of investing. In addition, no income tax liability of any kind has been paid. Thus, when looking at historical average rates of return, investors should be aware that the vast majority of investors received a lower return because of the impact of these other considerations.

Real Rates of Return—a More Recent Period

Now let's examine the real rates of return for a more recent period of history—the 25-year period from 1972 through 1996. Table 4-4 gives the real rates of return over inflation for Treasury bills, long-term government bonds, small-company stocks and S&P 500 Index stocks for this period. Later we will examine each year separately. The historical real rates of return from 1926 through 1996, and then from 1972 through 1996, can provide investors with a useful frame of reference when attempting to estimate future long-term real rates of return for their portfolios.

Table 4-4
Compound Rates of Return of Different Asset Classes, in Relation to Inflation, 1972-1996

Treasury Bills	7.0%
Inflation	-5.6%
Real Rate of Return	1.4%
Long-term Government Bonds	9.0%
Inflation	-5.6%
Real Rate of Return	3.4%
Large-company Stocks (S&P 500)	12.6%
Inflation	-5.6%
Real Rate of Return	7.0%
Small-company Stocks	13.9%
Inflation	-5.6%
Real Rate of Return	8.3%

In Table 4-4, investors in large-company stocks received a 7.0 percent real rate of return as compared to the 71-year real rate of return of 7.6 percent (Table 4-3). Investors in small-company stocks received an 8.3 percent real rate of return, compared with the historical 9.5 percent real rate of return for the period from 1926 through 1996. On the other hand, the real rate of return for long-term government bonds was substantially higher from 1972 through 1996 (3.4 percent) than from 1926 through 1996 (2.0 percent). The explanation for this increase in rates of return for long-term bonds (and their corresponding increase in volatility) is discussed in the next chapter on Volatility.

If we look at other periods of time for these asset classes, we can find both significantly higher and significantly lower real rates of return than the historical periods we have examined so far. For example, in the 10-year period from 1980 through 1989, investors in S&P 500 large-company stocks received an average compound rate of return of 17.5 percent, while inflation averaged 5.1 percent. Thus, these investors enjoyed a 12.4 percent real rate of return on large-company stocks—a rate significantly higher than both the 1926-1996 real rate of return of 7.6 percent and the 1972-1996 real rate of return of 7 percent.

Different Investment Periods

We have used charts to illustrate the historical real rates of return from 1926 through 1996 and from 1972 through 1996. We also saw that from 1980 to 1990 the real rate of return for the S&P 500 was 12.4 percent. However, there have been four 20-year periods when the real rate of return for the S&P 500 was under 2 percent. In fact, as recently as the 20-year period ending in December 1981, the S&P 500 produced a real rate of return of under 1 percent. If someone had invested 100 percent of his portfolio in the S&P 500 during that 20 year period, he would have been shocked by this dismal real rate of return.

Even if we recognize the importance of long-term real rates of return, what we see reported in print and electronic media and emphasized in financial advertisements are returns on investments before inflation. It's hard to think of real rates of returns when all we see and hear about are returns earned this month, this year or even this decade. This noise can cause even the most focused investors to make unrealistic assumptions regarding critical decisions about retirement, investments and other long-term financial planning.

A 25-Year History, Year by Year

The period from 1972 through 1996 includes the most recent time segment in U.S. history in which investors experienced a prolonged down market for both large- and small-company stocks. This period also saw years of double-digit inflation (reaching as high as 13.3 percent) and years when inflation sank below its historical average of 3.1 percent. It encompasses years when the returns of small-company stocks rose up to a positive 65.7 percent and fell to a negative 39 percent; and a year when the S&P 500 had a *negative 38.7 percent real rate of return*. Rates of return for long-term government bonds during this period ranged from a positive 40.4 percent to a negative 7.8 percent. The period offers investors a unique opportunity to carefully examine the effects of a broad range of market and economic conditions.

Tables 4-5 through 4-8 list year-by-year rates of return, inflation rates, and real rates of return for large-company U.S. stocks, small-company U.S. stocks, long-term government bonds and Treasury bills. Take the time to look at each asset class and its accompanying rates during the 25-year period. This can provide a clearer picture of what you might personally experience as an investor when you live through years of incredibly high returns, prolonged down markets, and runaway inflation. It also provides a look at those years in which investors endured negative real rates of return (as illustrated by the shaded boxes).

Table 4-5
Treasury Bills, Year-by-year Rates for 1972-1996
Note: Parentheses signify negative real rates of return

Year	Rate of Return	Inflation Rate	Real Rate of Return
1972	3.8%	3.4%	0.4%
1973	6.9%	8.8%	(1.9%)
1974	8.0%	12.2%	(4.2%)
1975	5.8%	7.0%	(1.2%)
1976	5.1%	4.8%	0.3%
1977	5.1%	6.8%	(1.7%)
1978	7.2%	9.0%	(1.8%)
1979	10.4%	13.3%	(2.9%)
1980	11.3%	12.4%	(1.1%)
1981	14.7%	8.9%	5.8%
1982	10.5%	3.9%	6.6%
1983	8.8%	3.8%	5.0%
1984	9.8%	4.0%	5.8%
1985	7.7%	3.8%	3.9%
1986	6.2%	1.1%	5.1%
1987	5.5%	4.4%	1.1%
1988	6.4%	4.4%	2.0%
1989	8.4%	4.6%	3.8%
1990	7.8%	6.1%	1.7%
1991	5.6%	3.1%	2.5%
1992	3.5%	3.0%	0.5%
1993	2.9%	2.8%	0.1%
1994	3.9%	2.7%	1.2%
1995	5.6%	2.7%	2.9%
1996	5.2%	3.3%	1.9%
AVERAGE	7.0%	5.6%	1.4%

Table 4-6
Long-term Government Bonds, Year-by-year Rates for 1972-1996
NOTE: Parentheses signify negative real rates of return

Year	Rate of Return	Inflation Rate	Real Rate of Return
1972	5.7%	3.4%	2.3%
1973	(1.1%)	8.8%	(9.9%)
1974	4.4%	12.2%	(7.8%)
1975	9.2%	7.0%	2.2%
1976	16.8%	4.8%	12.0%
1977	(0.7%)	6.8%	(7.5%)
1978	(1.2%)	9.0%	(10.2%)
1979	(1.2%)	13.3%	(14.5%)
1980	(4.0%)	12.4%	(16.4%)
1981	1.9%	8.9%	(7.0%)
1982	40.4%	3.9%	36.5%
1983	0.7%	3.8%	(3.1%)
1984	15.5%	4.0%	11.5%
1985	31.0%	3.8%	27.2%
1986	24.5%	1.1%	23.4%
1987	(2.7%)	4.4%	(7.1%)
1988	9.7%	4.4%	5.3%
1989	18.1%	4.6%	13.5%
1990	6.2%	6.1%	0.1%
1991	19.3%	3.1%	15.2%
1992	9.4%	3.0%	6.4%
1993	18.2%	2.8%	15.4%
1994	7.8%	2.7%	(10.5%)
1995	31.2%	2.7%	28.5%
1996	(0.9%)	3.3%	(4.2%)
AVERAGE	9.0%	5.6%	3.4%

Table 4-7
Large-company Stocks, Year-by-year Rates for 1972-1996

NOTE: Parentheses signify negative real rates of return

Year	Rate of Return	Inflation Rate	Real Rate of Return
1972	19.0%	3.4%	15.6%
1973	(14.7%)	8.8%	(23.5%)
1974	(26.5%)	12.2%	(38.7%)
1975	37.2%	7.0%	30.2%
1976	23.9%	4.8%	19.1%
1977	(7.2%)	6.8%	(14.0%)
1978	6.6%	9.0%	(2.4%)
1979	18.4%	13.3%	5.1%
1980	32.4%	12.4%	20.0%
1981	(4.9%)	8.9%	(13.8%)
1982	21.4%	3.9%	17.5%
1983	22.5%	3.8%	18.7%
1984	6.3%	4.0%	2.3%
1985	32.2%	3.8%	28.4%
1986	18.5%	1.1%	17.4%
1987	5.2%	4.4%	0.8%
1988	16.8%	4.4%	12.4%
1989	31.5%	4.6%	26.9%
1990	(3.2%)	6.1%	(9.3%)
1991	30.6%	3.1%	27.5%
1992	7.7%	3.0%	4.7%
1993	10.0%	2.8%	7.2%
1994	1.3%	2.7%	(1.4%)
1995	37.4%	2.7%	34.7%
1996	23.1%	3.3%	19.8%
AVERAGE	12.6%	5.6%	7.0%

Table 4-8
Small-company Stocks, Year-by-year Rates for 1972-1996

Note: Parentheses signify negative real rates of return

Year	Rate of Return	Inflation Rate	Real Rate of Return
1972	(0.3%)	3.4%	(3.7%)
1973	(39.0%)	8.8%	(47.8%)
1974	(28.7%)	12.2%	(40.9%)
1975	65.7%	7.0%	58.7%
1976	51.1%	4.8%	46.3%
1977	26.8%	6.8%	20.0%
1978	25.8%	9.0%	16.8%
1979	43.2%	13.3%	29.9%
1980	41.9%	12.4%	29.5%
1981	(2.7%)	8.9%	(11.6%)
1982	24.3%	3.9%	20.4%
1983	33.8%	3.8%	30.0%
1984	(11.6%)	4.0%	(15.6%)
1985	26.2%	3.8%	22.4%
1986	3.5%	1.1%	2.4%
1987	(14.2%)	4.4%	(18.6%)
1988	19.9%	4.4%	15.5%
1989	8.2%	4.6%	3.6%
1990	(28.0%)	6.1%	(34.1%)
1991	51.6%	3.1%	48.5%
1992	26.0%	3.0%	23.0%
1993	19.9%	2.8%	17.1%
1994	(2.3%)	2.7%	(5.0%)
1995	33.3%	2.7%	30.6%
1996	17.6%	3.3%	14.3%
AVERAGE	13.9%	5.6%	8.3%

Lump Sums Needed for Different Time Horizons

Now that we have reviewed the historical real rates of return of certain asset classes, let's use various real rates of return to estimate the lump sums of capital necessary for retirement or other long-term financial goals. Table 4-9 identifies the lump-sum amount you would need for every $10,000 stream of inflation-adjusted annual income, for different lengths of time, using real rates of return ranging from 8 percent to 1 percent. It assumes that all assets will be depleted at the end of the term. But unlike the charts most investors see, Table 4-9 is not concerned with whether you think that inflation in the long-term future will average 10 percent or 1 percent per year. It is only concerned with the real rate of return—the difference between your estimated return and the estimated inflation rate.

For example, to estimate how large a lump sum of capital you'll need for an inflation-adjusted $10,000 yearly income stream for 20 years in retirement, with an assumed real rate of return of 4 percent, you simply look in the second row (20 years) and the sixth column (4 percent) of Table 4-9; the answer is approximately $132,000. To calculate the lump sum needed to provide $30,000 per year of inflation-adjusted income for 20 years, multiply the $132,000 by 3; a lump sum of $396,000 is required. This lump sum would be what you would want to have accumulated by the first day of your retirement.

Table 4-9
Lump Sums Needed to Provide $10,000 Inflation-Adjusted Income Stream for Different Time Horizons at Various Real Rates of Return

No. of Years	Real Rate of Return (Actual Return less Inflation)			
	8%	7%	6%	5%
15	$86,000	$91,000	$97,000	$104,000
20	$96,000	$104,000	$112,000	$121,000
25	$105,000	$115,000	$125,000	$138,000
30	$111,000	$122,000	$135,000	$154,000
35	$116,000	$128,000	$143,000	$161,000
40	$118,000	$132,000	$149,000	$169,000

No. of Years	Real Rate of Return (Actual Return less Inflation)			
	4%	3%	2%	1%
15	$111,000	$119,000	$128,000	$139,000
20	$132,000	$144,000	$158,000	$193,000
25	$152,000	$169,000	$189,000	$212,000
30	$169,000	$191,000	$217,000	$249,000
35	$183,000	$210,000	$242,000	$283,000
40	$194,000	$226,000	$266,000	$317,000

Note: Numbers are rounded. This table assumes that all assets will be depleted at the end of the term. Underlying inflation rate used is a hypothetical 4.5 percent; to obtain an 8% real rate of return, an investor would have to earn 12.5% average actual compound return for the entire time period. All amounts are pre-tax.

Suppose as a couple, you want to save enough capital at retirement to provide $40,000 in inflation-adjusted income annually for 25 years, and you expect to achieve a 6 percent real rate of return.

By referring to row 3, column 4 of Table 4-9, you'll find that you need a lump sum of $125,000 for each $10,000 inflation-adjusted income stream; multiplying that number by 4 yields a figure of $500,000. Likewise, an investor who wants to plan for 30 years of retirement and expects a 2 percent real rate of return would have to accumulate a lump sum of $217,000 for each $10,000 stream of annual income needed.

A More Conservative Investment Portfolio in Retirement

Many investors plan to reduce or significantly limit the percentage of equities in their portfolios and become more conservative investors during their retirement years. But history has shown that more conservative portfolios bring lower real rates of return. Let's examine what this might mean for someone attempting to estimate the lump sum needed to provide a desired inflation-adjusted income stream during retirement.

We used an example above of a couple who wanted to estimate the lump sum necessary to provide a $40,000 yearly inflation-adjusted income stream for 25 years in retirement. At an assumed 6 percent real rate of return, they needed to accumulate a $500,000 lump sum. Now that they have reached retirement, they want to reduce the proportion of equities in their portfolio. But this desire creates the following dilemma: is it possible for them to achieve their goal of a more conservative portfolio during retirement and still reasonably expect to earn a real rate of return of 6 percent?

Addressing this couple's question raises the important issue of what is a reasonable expected real rate of return for any portfolio or asset class over an extended period of time. For example, would it be realistic to assume that the S&P 500 (large-company) stocks over the long term will earn a 12.4 percent real rate of return as they did in the decade of the 80's? Would it be reasonable, when investing in a mutual fund having a phenomenal track record over the past 15 years, to expect it to maintain the same level of performance in the future?

As we discussed earlier, using short-term periods could make investors quite vulnerable to overly optimistic or pessimistic expectations. Thus, most advisors look to an extended period of history of the real rates of return for the asset class or classes that have been selected for the portfolio and then try to project a reasonable real rate of return.

Based on the historical real rates of return illustrated in Tables 4-3 and 4-4, it may not be realistic for our couple to expect to earn a 6 percent real rate of return throughout retirement without investing a significant portion of their portfolio in equities. Since the couple wants to reduce the amount of equities in their portfolio—to be more conservative—a lower real rate of return should be expected. What if the expected real rate of return is reduced from 6 percent to 4 percent? The lump sum needed to provide an inflation-adjusted $40,000 annual income stream for 25 years at a 4 percent real rate of return would increase by more than 20 percent over the 6 percent real return figure, from $500,000 to $608,000. A 2 percent real rate of return would require a lump sum of $756,000. Because many investors desire lower risk investing during retirement, significantly lower expected real rates of return will be more realistic.

In our examples, the couple planned for a 25-year period of retirement. But most individuals underestimate how long they will live, which will have the same impact as a couple overestimating their expected real rate of return.

Outliving Your Assets?

It is important for investors to be extremely careful when estimating the lump sums they need for retirement. In my experience, many investors either underestimate the number of years they will live in retirement or overestimate the real rate of return they will receive during their retirement years.

The joint life expectancy of most couples today (that is, the age at which the one who outlives the other will die) is approximately 90 years of age. This statistic can be quite misleading, however, because it is *only an average.* Approximately 50 percent of the time one person in every couple will live beyond age 90, as we will discuss in the Time Horizons chapter. In addition, investors today tend to overestimate their expected real rate of return, because it has been more than 20 years since the last prolonged down stock market (1973-74). Even if you expect to reduce spending toward the latter part of your retirement years, the terrible truth is this: if you either underestimate the length of your retirement or overestimate your real rate of return, you take the risk of outliving your assets.

As Table 4-9 makes clear, the lower your real rate of return during retirement or the longer your retirement, the larger the lump sum you'll need for each $10,000 stream of yearly inflation-adjusted income you wish to provide for yourself in retirement. The table also serves as an important reminder that, when attempting to estimate the lump sum necessary for retirement at a desired level of annual income, the investment policy you plan to adopt after retirement has enormous financial consequences.

A More Aggressive Investment Portfolio in Retirement

Many investors, who better understand historical real rates of return and the length of time they will be investors in retirement, may conclude that they need to have a larger exposure to stocks in their retirement portfolios. At the same time, they must remind themselves of the numerous 20-year periods of time in which large-company stocks earned very low returns in relation to inflation. The retired investor who chooses a higher exposure to stocks must be aware that historically, *accepting additional risk has not always yielded a higher real rate of return.*

The expected outcomes of your investments can never be certain, regardless of how diligent you are in making your estimates. The question of how to better prepare ourselves for this uncertainty is addressed in the Selected Issues chapter when we discuss Monte Carlo simulation and lifecycle investing.

Taxes: The Not-So-Silent Embezzler

In trying to make sure that your investments adequately cover your future cost of living plus inflation, you cannot afford to ignore another embezzler: taxes. Earlier we calculated the lump sum needed to produce an inflation-adjusted $10,000 annual income stream at differing real rates of return and for differing lengths of retirement. But none of those calculations considered income taxes. Because most investors will draw some of their retirement income from tax-deferred accounts such as company-sponsored pension plans, 401(k) plans, or IRAs, let's use them as an example. Because these earnings are only tax-deferred, not tax free, the government has not been totally benevolent, just patient. When you start withdrawing your retirement assets, Uncle Sam insists on being paid his share.

Does 1+1 Always Equal Two?

If you knew you were in a 35 percent tax bracket and you wanted $10,000 spendable (after-tax) dollars, how much would you have to withdraw from your IRA, 401(k) or other retirement plan to receive this amount? Instinctively, you might visualize withdrawing $13,500 to net $10,000. However, you would have to withdraw $15,400, not $13,500, to net $10,000 at a tax rate of 35 percent. This means you, as an investor, must accumulate an astounding 54 percent more money to net the desired spendable $10,000.

Table 4-10 illustrates, at varying tax rates, how much you would have to withdraw from a retirement account to net $10,000. For example, if your tax rate was 15 percent, you would have to withdraw $11,800 and pay $1,800 in taxes, to have $10,000 to spend on goods and services. Tax rates vary from investor to investor. But as this chart clearly demonstrates, the tax burden, even at the lowest tax rates, is enormous.

Table 4-10
Amount Needed to Net $10,000 in Spendable (After-Tax) Income

Tax Rate	Pretax Withdrawal	Taxes Due	After-Tax Spendable Amount	Additional Amount Needed in %
15%	$11,800	$1,800	$10,000	18.0%
25%	$13,400	$3,400	$10,000	34.0%
35%	$15,400	$5,400	$10,000	54.0%
45%	$18,200	$8,200	$10,000	82.0%

Note: Amounts are rounded

Now let's see how income taxes might increase the lump sums needed for retirement. Suppose that a retiree is in a 35 percent tax bracket after retirement. Table 4-11 illustrates that at a tax rate of 35 percent, the lump sum needed increases from $132,000 to $211,000—a 52 percent increase. In other words, the retiree in our example must set aside $211,000 to provide an annual inflation-adjusted, *after-tax* income stream of $10,000 for 20 years.

Table 4-11 also illustrates the lump sum needed at other income tax rates and lengths of retirement. Here we are looking at tax rates after retirement; that is, this table addresses the question, what would it cost to produce an after-tax annual income of $10,000 for 20-, 25-, 30- and 35-year periods if all withdrawals from the portfolio were fully taxable at the differing tax rates?

Table 4-11
Lump Sums Needed to Provide Inflation-adjusted Spendable (After-Tax) Income of $10,000 per Year at a 4% Real Rate of Return

Tax Rate	Lump Sum Needed Without Taxes	Lump Sum Needed Including Taxes
20 Years		
0%	$132,000	$132,000
15%	$132,000	$156,000
25%	$132,000	$177,000
35%	$132,000	$203,000
45%	$132,000	$240,000
25 Years		
0%	$152,000	$152,000
15%	$152,000	$180,000
25%	$152,000	$204,000
35%	$152,000	$234,000
45%	$152,000	$277,000
30 Years		
0%	$169,000	$169,000
15%	$169,000	$199,000
25%	$169,000	$226,000
35%	$169,000	$260,000
45%	$169,000	$308,000
35 Years		
0%	$183,000	$183,000
15%	$183,000	$216,000
25%	$183,000	$245,000
35%	$183,000	$282,000
45%	$183,000	$333,000

Note: Amounts are rounded. And remember, in order to get a 4% real rate of return after costs, based on historic returns, most investors would need a higher concentration of equities in their portfolios throughout retirement than they expected.

Obviously, the higher the tax rate, the greater the lump-sum of money needed to produce an after-tax, inflation-adjusted $10,000 annual spendable income stream. But since the length of time a person needs money for retirement or other goals and the person's expected real rate of return and tax brackets differ, the dollars necessary to provide the income stream will vary.

So far, our examples have assumed that the income streams are coming from 401(k)s, company-sponsored retirement plans, or other tax-deferred accounts—moneys that are taxable when withdrawn. We have not taken into consideration personal assets that an individual has accumulated for retirement. In most instances, a person who has saved assets outside tax-deferred retirement accounts will need a somewhat smaller lump sum, since a portion of the assets to be withdrawn during retirement has already been taxed. Or, it is possible that withdrawal of some personal assets may enjoy favorable tax treatment, such as long-term capital gains. Under current law, investments held for 12 months or longer and then sold for a gain will be taxed at a lower rate than ordinary income. However, given the tax-free compounding of tax-deferred plans and the enormous lump sums needed to provide inflation-adjusted streams of income, investors should always consider taking advantage of tax-deferred qualified retirement plans.

Tax Rates at Retirement

Many investors base their investment strategies on the idea that they will be in a lower income tax bracket after retirement than during their working years. For some, this scenario occurs; for others, it does not. Changes in income tax laws and tax rates occur regularly and make it dangerous for investors to rely on any fixed set of assumptions. In addition, tax deductions for investors may change over time. For example, many people plan to have their house paid off by the time they retire, or they may choose to downsize and live in more modest housing. In either case, investors would have less mortgage interest to deduct as an offset to taxable income. Furthermore, inflationary increases may artificially push taxpayers into higher tax brackets.

No one can predict future income tax rates, as rates have fluctuated through history. Table 4-12 illustrates how the maximum ordinary income tax rates for each year have varied from 1934 to the present. They do not include lower tax rates connected with long-term capital gains or any other favorable tax treatment.

Table 4-12
Maximum Federal Income Tax Rates, 1934–1997

Years in Effect	Maximum Tax Rate
1934-1935	63%
1936-1940	79%
1941	81%
1942-1943	88%
1944-1945	90%
1946-1947	85.5%
1948-1949	77%
1950	80%
1951	87.2%
1952-1953	88%
1954-1963	87%
1964	77%
1965-1981	70%
1982-1986	50%
1987	38.5%
1988-1991	33%
1992	31%
1993—1997	39.6%

Can Lower Tax Rates Mean More Taxes?

Table 4-12 indicates that after 1981, maximum ordinary income tax rates went down substantially. What the table does not show is that today a larger percentage of many individuals' income is taxed than ever before. For example, Social Security taxes have substantially increased, interest on consumer debt is no longer deductible, tax shelters that were once available have been eliminated and the government has quietly phased out for many taxpayers other itemized deductions and personal exemptions.

Summary: Tools for the Savvy Investor

A comprehensive understanding of real rates of return can serve as a foundation for making better investment decisions.

- Favorable short-term rates of return may give you something to brag about; but knowing realistic long-term real rates of return give you something you can use: the ability to realistically determine how much money you need to retire.

- Understanding the relationship between inflation and historical rates of return earned by different asset classes can help you avoid unrealistic expectations about your real rates of return when you choose investments.

- Examining the year-by-year returns and inflation rates from 1972 through 1996 gives you the opportunity to observe up and down markets and high and low inflation, which in turn can help prepare you to weather market conditions you may confront as a long-term investor.

- Taxes, even at lower brackets, place an enormous burden on your ability to retire. Understanding the size of this burden makes it less likely you will underestimate the lump sum of money needed for retirement or other long-term financial goals.

- The lower the real rate of return or the longer a retirement, the larger the lump sum of money that must be accumulated. This can help you understand the importance of formulating a long-term investment strategy that will serve you from today through the end of your retirement years.

RISK AND
VOLATILITY

Some Terrible Truths

- Many investors believe they can avoid risk.

- Few investors have experienced the personal agony of a prolonged down stock market.

- Investors who don't understand risk may react emotionally to normal market fluctuations.

- Sophisticated investors think that they are prepared to weather long-term declining stock markets, but history has proved otherwise.

- Many investors think the stock market crashed in 1987.

In an earlier chapter we examined the history of returns of some major asset classes, such as large- and small-company stocks, long-term government bonds and Treasury bills. We found, for example, that large-company stocks of the S&P 500 Index earned an average annual compound return of 10.7 percent from 1926 through 1996, and that small stocks earned 12.6 percent over the same period.

However, looking at these returns alone tells only part of the story. We also need to look at the extreme statistical and emotional swings investors had to endure to earn those returns.

The moment you invest money, you subject yourself to some kind of risk. There are different kinds of risk, including:

- the risk that inflation will erode your ability to buy the same goods and services in the future; and

- the risk of uncertainty and unpredictability you take with investments that attempt to get higher rates of return.

When investors attempt to get higher returns, they subject themselves to uncertain and unpredictable investments that fluctuate up and down. These fluctuations are called *volatility*. Volatility is the change in value of an investment (up or down), which occurs on a daily, monthly or yearly basis. If history is a reliable guide, the range of these fluctuations will vary dramatically, depending on the type of investment.

When most investors think about volatility, they usually think of stocks. However, we will see that fixed-income investments, such as long-term bonds, subject investors to significant volatility as well. Of course, investors rarely notice volatility while their investments are substantially increasing in value. But they are keenly aware of volatility when they see their investments decrease in value or when they suffer a loss once they sell them.

When the subject of the volatility of stock markets is raised, most investors remember the so-called "Crash of 1987." On October 19, 1987, the Dow Jones Industrial Average suddenly plummeted 508 points, losing nearly 25 percent of its value. It was the largest single-day percentage drop in the history of the U.S. stock market. This particular down market lasted less than 90 days. However, other down markets have lasted for many months, quarters, even years. During prolonged down markets, investors have been known to abandon hope of ever seeing positive returns again. This feeling was widespread during the Depression, the down market of 1973 through 1974, and other extended down periods.

In This Chapter...

We will review the enormous ups and downs in the value of large- and small-company stocks and long-term bonds. Chances are, you will then conclude that historically, investments have been much more volatile than you thought. Review can also provide some insight into the enormous ranges of returns or volatility investors might expect from these asset classes in the future. By better understanding the radical fluctuations in value that investors have been subjected to historically, you can ask yourself, "Would I have been able to endure the type of market fluctuations that were necessary to obtain these returns?" By exploring the critical role that human nature and emotions play in the investment process—a role too often overlooked in discussions of investment volatility and risk—you may be better prepared to live with the volatility inherent in the investments you choose in attempting to meet your investment goals.

It may be surprising to see how irrationally some institutional investors reacted to the last prolonged down market of 1973 through 1974. In this chapter we will examine month by month what would have happened to a hypothetical investment over that two-year period—and find a graphic picture of the punishment and stress investors had to endure.

We will also look at questionnaires that are often used to help investors determine how much risk they can tolerate when developing their portfolio of investments, and we will investigate whether these questions go far enough. In addition, we will ask the question: was there truly a stock market crash in 1987?

Why Invest in Volatile Assets?

Earlier, we examined inflation and the tremendous challenge it poses when investors attempt to accumulate the assets necessary to retire. Many investors deal with this challenge by selecting investments they expect will provide higher real rates of return over inflation. Such rates may be necessary not only to accumulate the assets needed to retire, but to preserve the purchasing power of those assets after retirement. However, higher real rates of return almost always come with a price tag: higher levels of volatility.

Let's compare volatility to a medical problem. Your physician has determined that you suffer from a chronic condition. She tells you about a medication for treating this condition but says it has side effects that can range from quite severe in some patients to mild in others, no matter what the dosage. But without medication, your physician says your condition will eventually worsen.

Your "chronic condition" is inflation; the "medication" consists of various types of investments that have higher expected rates of return over inflation; and the "side effects" are volatility and the lack of a guaranteed reward. Investors are faced with a dilemma. Do you try to live with the original condition—the risk of inflation—or do you swallow the medication for higher expected returns and accept the side effects of volatility and uncertainty?

A proper understanding of volatility and risk can assist you in a number of ways. It can help you better evaluate the level of risk in your portfolio's investments. It can also help you or your advisor select investments that are more suitable for you, or design a less volatile combination of asset classes in your portfolio, which may increase the chances of staying committed to your investment strategy over the long term. And finally, an appreciation of volatility can help you minimize the dangerous role that emotions play in investing.

The Side Effects of "Medication"

For some investors, the "medication" of higher-risk investments could prove to be worse than the original condition of inflation. For example, investors who cannot tolerate market volatility and who react by selling any of their investments that decline in value could be better off financially by avoiding the medication altogether. Also, an investor who has chosen more volatile investments but has never watched his investments decline in value has not truly experienced the kind of emotional trauma that can arise when attempting to earn higher returns.

A Place to Start

In the Investment Fundamentals and Historical Returns chapter, we looked at the historical rates of return of various asset classes from 1926-1996 and saw that small-company U.S. stocks had an average annual compound return of 12.6 percent; large-company U.S. stocks (S&P 500) averaged 10.7 percent; long-term government bonds averaged 5.1 percent; and Treasury bills averaged 3.7 percent. Let's examine each of these asset classes to see how much volatility investors had to endure in order to get such returns.

Large-company U.S. Stocks

As previously mentioned, the S&P 500 Index consists of the stocks of large publicly traded corporations in the U.S. From 1926 through 1996, this asset class had an average annual compound return of 10.7 percent. "Average annual compound return" doesn't mean these stocks had a 10.7 percent return every year—far from it. In fact, from year to year the returns on this asset class varied quite significantly from this number. The single highest annual return during this period was a gain of 54 percent, and the single lowest annual return was a loss of 43 percent—an incredible 97 percentage point differential! Chart 5-1 gives us an excellent snapshot of just how volatile the yearly returns of the S&P 500 were during this 71-year period. *You can see that investors took quite a dramatic ride to obtain that 10.7 percent average!*

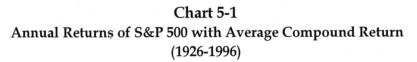

Chart 5-1
Annual Returns of S&P 500 with Average Compound Return
(1926-1996)

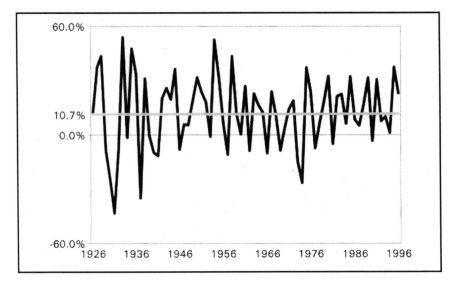

Standard Deviation: Measuring the Risk

To better understand the volatility an investor would have had to experience to receive that 10.7 percent compound return, let's define *standard deviation*. Standard deviation is a number that tells how much the annual returns vary, up or down, two-thirds of the time, from the average return. The S&P 500's average annual compound return was 10.7 percent, and its historical standard deviation was 20.3 percent. This means that returns fluctuated by 20.3 percentage points above and below the historical 10.7 percent return, two-thirds of the time. In other words, historical returns ranged from a positive 31 percent (the 10.7 percent compound return plus the 20.3 percent standard deviation) to a negative 9.6 percent (10.7 percent minus the 20.3 percent standard deviation) about two-thirds of the time.

NOTE: *Throughout this book we have used compound returns. However, standard deviation is more commonly computed on the basis of average returns. For the sake of consistency, though, we use compound returns when computing standard deviation ranges in this chapter. If you are interested in the difference between average and compound returns, see the explanation of those terms in the Glossary.*

The Necessity of Understanding Standard Deviation

Trying to understand standard deviation can be compared to programming your VCR for the first time. Many people find standard deviation difficult to comprehend, and even those who understand it can still find it confusing to explain. Clearly understanding standard deviation, however, is extremely valuable, since it can help us see the kind of risk investors have historically faced when they select different types of investments. Also, it can better prepare investors for the volatility they may encounter in the future.

Chart 5-2 shows the historical compound return drawn at 10.7 percent. Now let's take this 10.7 percent and add the standard deviation of 20.3 percent, which equals a positive 31 percent, and draw a horizontal line there. Then from the historical compound 10.7 percent, let's subtract the standard deviation of 20.3 percent, which equals a negative 9.6 percent, and draw another horizontal line there. The range between the lines at positive 31 percent and negative 9.6 percent is the measure of the historical volatility of the S&P 500, approximately two-thirds of the time.

Chart 5-2
Annual Returns of S&P 500 with Standard Deviation Range
(1926-1996)

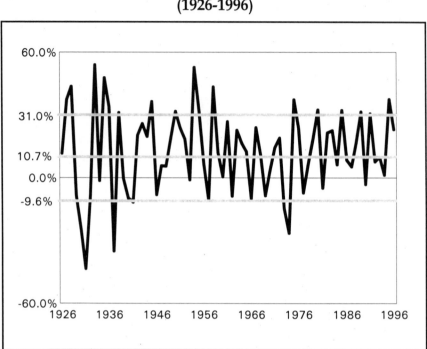

Measuring the Range

Now let's reconsider the range of returns in Chart 5-2. If we shade in the area between the lines at positive 31 percent and negative 9.6 percent, as shown in Chart 5-3, you can see more clearly that this shaded area captures roughly two-thirds of the annual returns for the S&P 500 over the 71-year period. The overall range of volatility, which is captured by the shaded area, encompasses all the returns between a positive 31 percent and a negative 9.6 percent, or 40.6 percentage points. In other words, investors experienced a variation in annual returns within a 40.6 percentage point range, two-thirds of the time.

Chart 5-3
Annual Returns of S&P 500 with Shaded Range of Returns
(1926-1996)

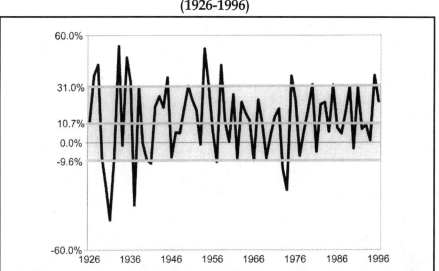

We also see that the returns during certain years lie outside the shaded area—either above the upper boundary or below the lower one. These are the years when investment returns exceeded 31 percent and the years when the loss was more than 9.6 percent.

Two-thirds of the Time

Because a key element of the definition of *standard deviation* requires us to think in terms of ranges of historical returns *two-thirds of the time*, let's define what this means. Visualize rolling a die (one of a pair of dice). A die has six sides, so we will let the numbers 2, 3, 4 and 5 represent two-thirds of the sides of the die, and the numbers 1 and 6 represent the other one-third of the sides.

Picture yourself rolling the die and getting a 2, 3, 4 or 5. If you do, your return for that year for large-company stocks will fall within the historical range of the standard deviation—that is, inside the lines of a positive 31 percent to a negative 9.6 percent, as indicated on

Charts 5-2 and 5-3. If, instead, you roll a 1 or a 6, your return for that year will fall outside the range—either above or below the shaded area.

Just as you can't predict what number your die will roll each time, you can't know in advance what investment performance you'll get each year. In addition, "two-thirds of the time" does not mean the return will fall within this range in two out of *every* three years: this average emerges only over time. You get the average *only on a random basis* two-thirds of the time. Picture yourself rolling the die over and over again. You know if you roll it six times, it is unlikely you will get a 1, 2, 3, 4, 5 and 6. Since the die has no memory, you easily could roll a 6 a couple of times in a row.

It's Out of Your Hands

We've all played games using dice, such as Monopoly. There are times when rolling a certain number can win the game for you. If you concentrate on rolling a specific number and succeed, you naturally think that you have real skill! During that moment, it is easy to lose sight of the fact that each time you roll the dice, the outcome is a random result of a new set of probabilities.

The Best Way to Understand Volatility

Probably the best way to understand volatility and standard deviation is to consider what these concepts mean in dollars. Let's use $1,000 in our examples. At the beginning of the year you invest $1,000 in the large-company stocks, represented by the S&P 500. Remember, the historical returns for this asset class (as defined by the standard deviation) ranged from a negative 9.6 percent to a positive 31 percent two-thirds of the time. On January 1, you roll the die and get a 2, 3, 4 or 5. This means that when you look at your account on December 31, your investment will have a value of somewhere between $904 (a negative 9.6 percent return) and $1,310 (a positive 31 percent return). This range from a negative 9.6 percent to a positive 31 percent is quite dramatic. But, if you happen to roll a 1 or a 6, that would correspond to having more than $1,310 or less than

Investment	$1,000
Return (9.6%)	-96
	$ 904
Investment	$1,000
Return 31%	+310
	$1,310

$904 in your account on December 31—an even wider range.

What if on December 31 you looked at your account and saw that it held $1,060 (a 6 percent increase) or $940 (a 6 percent loss)? Either result would lie within the expected range of $904 to $1,310 as measured by standard deviation. The same is true of an investment worth $1,280 (a 28 percent increase) or $920 (an 8 percent loss) on December 31. All of these results are equivalent to having rolled a 2, 3, 4, or 5 on your die. If you understand the historical risk and volatility of this asset class, the range of returns described should not surprise you.

Next, suppose that at the end of the year your $1,000 was down a full 15 percent, so that your account had only $850. How would you feel? You may be anxious, concerned and disappointed. This could also come at a time when you are already feeling vulnerable because of some outside personal factors such as job insecurity, loss of a loved one, or personal stress. You may feel confused and want to make changes in your investments. You could find yourself asking people you know whether it is time to sell, or whether their accounts are down too. *Under these circumstances it is difficult to remember that you merely happened to roll a 1 or a 6.*

On the other hand, at the end of the year you may find that your investment had risen by 35 percent, so that your $1,000 has grown to $1,350. How would you feel? You may feel happy about your good fortune and proud of how your investment has performed. But once again, all that has happened is that you simply rolled a 1 or a 6.

Considering how easy it is to roll a 1 or a 6 any given time we roll a die—and remembering that each year brings a brand-new roll of the die—we should not be surprised when investment returns from large-company stocks fluctuate significantly from year to year. The goal is to say, "The real news is that I rolled a 1 or a 6." But as we will discuss later in this chapter, when we take into consideration the enormous role that emotions play in investing, it is hard to be so matter-of-fact.

Let's review the steps we have taken to understand the historical risk and volatility of the S&P 500. First, we obtained the historical compound return (10.7 percent) and the standard deviation (20.3 percent). Second, we added and subtracted the 20.3 percent standard deviation to the 10.7 percent compound return to establish upper and lower limits for a range of returns. Third, we shaded this range to show the overall range of volatility of 40.6 percentage points. Fourth, we translated the range of percentage returns into dollars. Table 5-1 summarizes this information.

Table 5-1
Historical Volatility of S&P 500 Stocks, 1926–1996

Average Annual Compound Return	10.7%
Standard Deviation	20.3%
Range of Returns	(9.6%) to 31.0%
Size of Range	40.6%
Translated into Dollars ($1,000 investment)	$904 to $1,310

A Favorable Past Can Make Us Vulnerable

Investors can be particularly vulnerable to normal market fluctuations, particularly down markets, if their experience with investments has only been favorable. For example, returns for the asset class of large-company stocks were positive in 19 out 22 years from 1976 through 1997, so investors did not experience much negative volatility. 401(k) plans first began to be widely used after 1982, but a 401(k) investor who was invested in the stocks of the S&P 500 Index during 1982 through 1997 (a 16-year period) would have experienced only one losing year. And that loss was only a negative 3.2 percent. Whether you are an advisor or investor, if your personal experience has been to almost always see your investments increase in value, it is simply human nature to expect that things will continue as they have in the past. In fact, investors always minimize the role volatility plays until they see the value of their investments decline.

Maybe the best way for those investors who have not experienced negative investment returns over long periods of time to understand their vulnerability is to draw upon experiences from other parts of their lives. Some have experienced long periods of time where things went well, but then events unexpectedly changed for the worse—a job disappeared, health declined, personal issues set in. Drawing upon difficult personal experiences helps investors to understand the kind of challenge they may face if markets decline, particularly over long periods.

Volatility Month by Month

Looking at the volatility of an asset class in yet another way may assist you in understanding risk. Let's look again at large-company U.S. stocks represented by the S&P 500 and examine the volatility of returns on a *monthly* basis, instead of using the annual returns we used in Charts 5-1, 5-2, and 5-3.

Monthly numbers may be closer to what individuals actually notice as they receive monthly mutual fund or brokerage statements. Investors can also track their investment values daily in the newspaper, over the Internet, or through 800 numbers, 24 hours a day. The media not only report market returns daily, but they often have live updates from the trading room floors throughout the day. Investors are thus more aware of the movements of financial markets over shorter periods of time than ever before in history.

Chart 5-4 illustrates the month-to-month fluctuations that produced the historical 10.7 percent annual compound return of the S&P 500 Index. This chart offers a vivid picture of the enormous volatility investors had to endure to earn this return. Even during the decade of the 1980s, when the annual compound return for large-company U.S. stocks averaged a remarkable 17.5 percent, investors experienced significant monthly volatility.

Chart 5-4
Volatility of S&P 500 Monthly Returns (1926-1996)

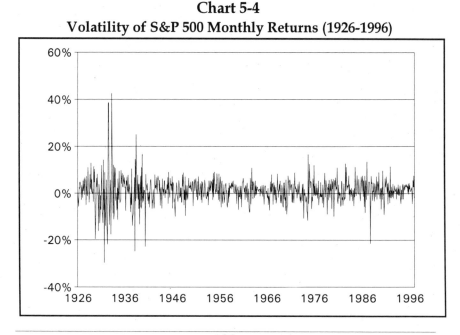

In fact, over this 71-year period, investors received negative monthly returns about 20 percent of the time—or roughly *one month out of five* (on a random basis). If Chart 5-4 looks traumatic, that's because it shows the fluctuations investors actually experienced month by month.

Other Asset Classes

Most individuals do not own just a single asset class. They may choose to diversify among other asset classes, such as small-company stocks, bonds, and real estate. Investors must focus on each asset class they own or are considering purchasing and understand its historical risk and volatility individually. Let's now look at two other asset classes—small-company U.S. stocks and long-term U.S. government bonds—and examine their historical risk and volatility.

Small-company U.S. Stocks

When we looked at small-company U.S. stocks in the Investment Fundamentals and Historical Returns chapter, we saw that their historical compound return from 1926 to 1996 was 12.6 percent, while the compound return of the S&P 500 was 10.7 percent. But once again, the 1.9 percentage points of additional return reveals only part of the story. What it does not disclose is the incredible level of volatility that investors in small-company stocks were subjected to in order to earn this additional return.

Chart 5-5 illustrates the annual returns for small-company U.S. stocks over a 71-year period, with a horizontal line drawn at the average annual compound return of 12.6 percent.

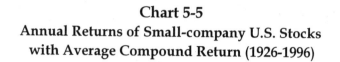

Chart 5-5
Annual Returns of Small-company U.S. Stocks
with Average Compound Return (1926-1996)

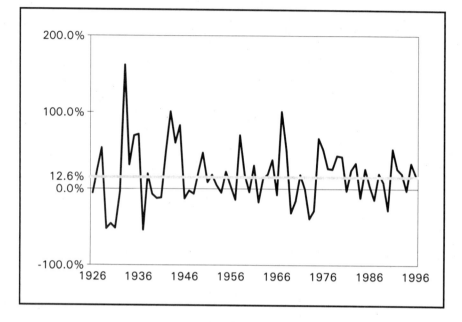

Highs, Lows and Averages

From 1926 through 1996 the highest return for a single year for the asset class of small-company stocks was an amazingly positive 143 percent, while the single lowest year was a distressingly negative 58 percent. Remember, these returns are the *average* of all the stocks represented in this asset class. Imagine the returns for individual stocks in the highest and lowest years that made up these averages. In those years, some stocks skyrocketed more than 5,000 percent while other companies simply went bankrupt.

Standard Deviation of Small-company Stocks

Let's go through the same steps as we did with the S&P 500 to understand the volatility of small-company U.S. stocks. The historical standard deviation for small-company stocks was 34.1 percent over the 71-year period of 1926-1996. Once again, we take the annual compound return of 12.6 percent and successively add and subtract the standard deviation. We find that the annual returns ranged from a positive 46.7 percent (12.6 percent plus 34.1 percent) to a negative 21.5 percent (12.6 percent minus 34.1 percent), two-thirds of the time.

Annual Return	**12.6**
+ Standard Deviation	**+34.1%**
Upper Limit of Range	**46.7%**
Annual Return	**12.6%**
- Standard Deviation	**-34.1%**
Lower Limit of Range	**(21.5%)**

In Chart 5-6, the historical range of returns for small-company stocks defined by the standard deviation has been shaded. You can see that the volatility of this asset class produced an enormous range of returns of 68.2 percentage points two-thirds of the time. The other one-third of the time, returns fell outside this range. Earlier, we pointed out that small-company stocks received an average annual compound return 1.9 percentage points higher than large-company stocks. *However, investors had to endure a staggering 70 percent increase in volatility in order to get that extra return.*

Chart 5-6
Annual Returns of Small-company U.S. Stocks
with Shaded Range of Returns (1926-1996)

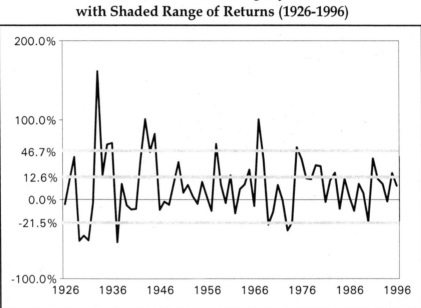

Converting to Dollars

Now let's convert the range of returns for small-company U.S. stocks into dollars. If at the beginning of the year you had invested $1,000 in small-company stocks and then rolled a 2, 3, 4, or 5, at the end of the year your account value would be anywhere from $785 (loss of 21.5 percent) to $1,467 (gain of 46.7 percent). If you happened to roll a 1 or a 6, your account value would be less than $785 or more than $1,467. Remember too, with each new year comes a new roll of the die. Table 5-2 summarizes the historical volatility for small-company stocks.

Table 5-2
Historical Volatility of Small-company U.S. Stocks (1926–1996)

Average Annual Compound Return	12.6%
Standard Deviation	34.1%
Range of Returns	(21.5%) to 46.7%
Size of Range	68.2%
Translated into Dollars ($1,000 investment)	$785 to $1,467

Monthly Volatility of Small-company Stocks

Once again, to better understand what investors had to endure in order to achieve this historical 12.6 percent return, let's look at the month-to-month volatility of small-company stocks. Chart 5-7 gives us a snapshot of the volatility of this asset class.

Chart 5-7
Volatility of Small-company U.S. Stocks
Monthly Returns (1926-1996)

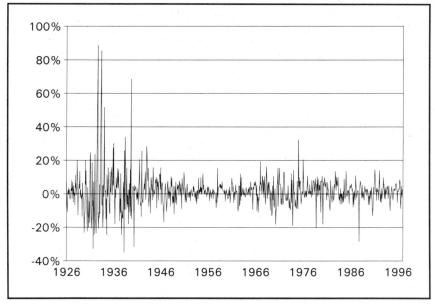

Volatility + Returns = Suitability

This review of the historical volatility of small-company stocks is an excellent reminder that you should understand not only the returns of every asset class you invest in but also look at its historical volatility. This can reduce your chances of overreacting to what could be the normal volatility of your investments. It also could keep you from selecting investments that are more volatile than you may care to own.

Volatility of Long-term U.S. Government Bonds

Annual Return	5.1%
+ Standard Deviation	+9.2%
Upper Limit of Range	14.3%
Annual Return	5.1%
- Standard Deviation	-9.2%
Lower Limit of Range	(4.1%)

Many investors believe that fixed income investments are relatively stable and predictable and, therefore, not volatile. Let's examine the volatility of long-term U.S. government bonds that have a maturity of 20 years and see if this is so.

From 1926 through 1996, these bonds had a compound return of 5.1 percent and a standard deviation of 9.2 percent. Again, we take the compound return of 5.1 percent and successively add the standard deviation of 9.2 percent (to get a positive 14.3 percent) and subtract it (to get a negative 4.1 percent). The volatility of this asset class produces an overall range of volatility of 18.4 percentage points, roughly two-thirds of the time.

Chart 5-8 illustrates the volatility for long-term U.S. government bonds, with a line drawn at its historical compound return of 5.1 percent. Further lines are drawn at 14.3 percent, and negative 4.1 percent. The shading indicates the 18.4 percentage point range of return investors experienced two-thirds of the time.

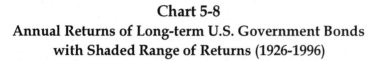

Chart 5-8
Annual Returns of Long-term U.S. Government Bonds
with Shaded Range of Returns (1926-1996)

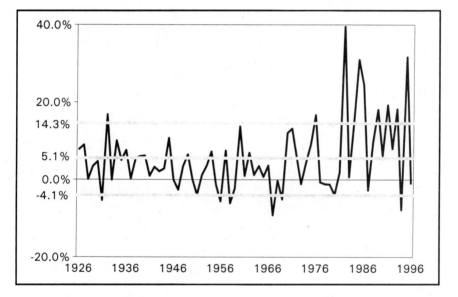

While the historical standard deviation of long-term U.S. government bonds from 1926 to 1996 was 9.2 percent, it is important to note that since 1970, the volatility of this asset class has increased significantly. The standard deviation from 1926 to 1969 was 5.3 percent. However, the standard deviation from 1970 to 1996 more than doubled, to 12 percent. Analysts have offered various explanations for this increase in volatility, including higher inflation, governmental deregulation of interest rates, freer markets that allowed foreign investment in U.S. government bonds, and the U.S. government's decision to go off the gold standard.

Converting to Dollars

Let's convert the standard deviation or volatility of this asset class into dollars. Suppose that on January 1 you invest $1,000 in long-term U.S. government bonds. If you roll a 2, 3, 4, or 5, your $1,000 account value on December 31 could be anywhere from $1,143 (gain of 14.3 percent) to $959 (loss of 4.1 percent); if you roll a 1 or a 6, your account value on December 31 may be less than $959 or more than $1,143. The statistics are shown in Table 5-3.

Table 5-3
Historical Volatility of Long-term U.S. Government Bonds (1926–1996)

Average Annual Compound Return	5.1%
Standard Deviation	9.2%
Range of Returns	(4.1%) to 14.3%
Size of Range	18.4%
Translated into Dollars ($1,000 investment)	$959 to $1,143

Monthly Volatility of Long-term U.S. Government Bonds

Looking at the returns of 20-year U.S. government bonds on a monthly basis in Chart 5-9 more clearly shows the volatility of this asset class. Even though government bonds guarantee investors their principal will be returned at maturity, we can see how the value of bonds changes from month to month in response to interest-rate fluctuations. Looking at this chart also gives us an opportunity to see just how much more volatile long-term government bonds have become over the last 25 years.

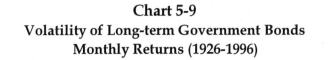

Chart 5-9
Volatility of Long-term Government Bonds
Monthly Returns (1926-1996)

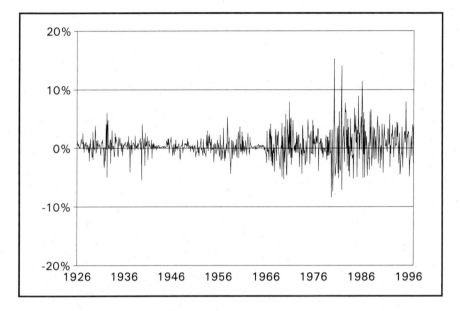

Prolonged Down Markets

An understanding of risk is more critical today than ever before. As this book went to press, the last prolonged down U.S. stock market occurred during 1973 through 1974, almost a generation ago. This truly significant market collapse has been generally ignored by the media and investors, even though it was second only to the stock market losses that accompanied the Great Depression of the 1930s.

Many investors today did not experience the 1973–1974 market collapse or had no significant assets invested at that time. Because they have not personally experienced watching their assets substantially decrease in value, they may not fully understand what risk and volatility can do to their portfolios.

Although there is no common definition of a "prolonged down market," most experts would agree that three calendar quarters in a row of negative market returns, or a total drop of at least 20 percent, constitute a "down" or "bear" market. From 1973 through 1974, both large- and small-company stocks in the U.S. generated negative returns for 6 of 8 quarters. During the first part of the Great Depression (from 1929 through 1932) large-company stocks produced negative returns in 10 of 16 quarters, and the value of small-company stocks declined in 12 of 16 quarters.

It is important to go back to the years of 1973 and 1974 to see what investors actually experienced when invested in the asset classes of large- and small-company U.S. stocks. For large-company stocks, we find that the returns for S&P 500 stocks declined by a total of 14.7 percent in 1973 and by 26.5 percent in 1974. Small-company stocks declined by 38.9 percent in 1973 and by 28.6 percent in 1974.

We have described this 1973-1974 prolonged down market in percentage terms. But to gain insight into what investors lived through, let's see what would have happened to a $1,000 investment in both large- and small-company stocks month by month over this 24-month period. Tables 5-4 and 5-5 illustrate the fluctuating monthly values in these hypothetical accounts. It is important for all investors, *and particularly for you if you had no investments during this period of time,* to assume that this hypothetical $1,000 is *your* money and see what you would have experienced during each month of this two year period.

Table 5-4
Tracking $1,000 Invested In Large-and Small-company Stocks
Month by Month in 1973

1973	Large-company Stocks		Small-company Stocks	
	Monthly Return	Value of Original $1,000	Monthly Return	Value of Original $1,000
January	(1.6%)	$984	(3.1%)	$969
February	(3.3%)	$952	(8.3%)	$889
March	0.0%	$952	(3.0%)	$862
April	(3.9%)	$914	(7.9%)	$794
May	(1.4%)	$902	(9.5%)	$718
June	(0.5%)	$897	(4.3%)	$688
July	3.9%	$932	12.0%	$770
August	(3.2%)	$902	(5.2%)	$730
September	4.1%	$939	8.2%	$790
October	0.0%	$939	(0.3%)	$788
November	(10.8%)	$838	(18.9%)	$639
December	1.8%	$853	(4.3%)	$612
YEARLY TOTAL	(14.7%)		(38.9%)	
VALUE OF $1,000 AT END OF FIRST YEAR		$853		$612

Table 5-5
Tracking $1,000 Invested in Large- and Small-company Stocks
Month by Month in 1974

	Large-company Stocks		Small-company Stocks	
1974	Monthly Return	Value of Original $1,000	Monthly Return	Value of Original $1,000
January	(0.8%)	$846	14.2%	$699
February	0.2%	$848	0.3%	$701
March	(2.2%)	$829	1.2%	$710
April	(3.7%)	$798	(5.8%)	$668
May	(2.7%)	$777	(7.8%)	$616
June	(1.3%)	$767	(3.4%)	$595
July	(7.6%)	$708	(5.7%)	$561
August	(8.3%)	$650	(8.7%)	$513
September	(11.7%)	$574	(7.5%)	$475
October	16.6%	$669	7.7%	$511
November	(4.5%)	$639	(6.0%)	$480
December	(1.8%)	$627	(9.0%)	$437
YEARLY TOTAL	(26.5%)		(28.6%)	
VALUE OF $1,000 AT END OF SECOND YEAR		$627		$437

The Devastation of Prolonged Down Markets

We have seen the monthly returns and their impact on an initial investment of $1,000 over this two-year period. Now let's consider the experience of an investor who had more money invested in stocks during that time. Picture yourself holding $100,000 worth of large-company stocks on December 31, 1972. Over the next 24 months, you watch this $100,000 decrease in value to $62,700. This is exactly what happened to the value of a portfolio invested in the S&P 500 from the beginning of 1973 through the last quarter of 1974. Or perhaps the $100,000 was invested in small-company stocks. At the end of 1974, your account was worth only $43,700.

Let's go back to 1973-74 and see how that down market devastated the value of some specific stocks. Avon Products plummeted from 140 to 18-5/8, Walt Disney dropped from 119-1/8 to 16-5/8, Polaroid fell from 149 to 14-1/8, and Xerox sank from 171 to 49. During this period, a group of stocks called the "Nifty Fifty" were the favorites of institutional investors because they represented blue-chip companies with proven records of growth and stability. They were widely held because it was thought they would weather poor markets without sacrificing potential long-term growth. The Nifty Fifty were supposed to be different from more speculative stocks. In fact, *the Nifty Fifty actually plummeted a staggering 80 percent in value from their peak.*

As the grim two years unfolded, some of the country's most prestigious financial publications printed story after story seriously questioning the future viability of investing in stocks. Were investors prepared for the psychological battering they experienced as a result of those devastating declines? Hardly. Many sophisticated institutional investors and managers of large pools of assets were unable to deal with the prolonged down market of 1973-74. They proved susceptible to panic and either radically changed or abandoned their long-standing investment policies, resulting in the loss of billions of dollars. The fledgling mutual fund industry was almost decimated. One of the largest and most respected trust companies in America stopped its buying of stocks entirely for its clients. This decision not to buy was not made solely on the basis that stocks had so dramatically declined in value, but also because it was felt that stocks were no longer considered suitable long-term investments. Other investors sharply cut back the portion of their investment portfolios that were invested in stocks.

In trying to understand the difficulty that even talented and highly experienced investors have had when faced with a prolonged down market, we must look to the significant role emotions can play. It would be like a longtime tennis player who has become quite proficient as a result of playing regularly and being a good student of the game. He consistently serves well, usually keeps the ball in play, even on difficult shots, and seldom loses a match. But suddenly, his game starts to fail him. First his serving becomes erratic and the ball often goes into the net. Then he is unable to keep the ball in play. Eventually, losing becomes the norm, and winning becomes the exception rather than the rule.

I have asked several proficient tennis players if this had ever happened to them. They all said it had. When I asked them how they felt, they said they had lost confidence in their game. When I asked how they might react if this had continued for a long period of time, the unanimous response was: "I would have seriously considered whether I should continue to play the game." Whether in sports, work, hobbies, or other areas of our lives where we have become proficient, long-term reversals generally lead to a loss of confidence. Once again we are reminded how emotions can influence our decisions and can understand how the professional money managers lost confidence in stocks during 1973-1974.

Like most money managers, investment counselors, stockbrokers, financial advisors, and investment journalists, most individual investors today began investing after 1974. As a result, they have limited personal experience with prolonged down stock markets. Likewise, few individuals participating in 401(k) plans that have invested in large-company stocks have experienced such declines; in the years from 1982 through 1997, only one year suffered a negative return for this asset class. Thus, most of today's investors have not been tested emotionally by the kind of continuous, long-term negative returns that have occurred and may occur again.

Even Seasoned Investors Make Emotional Decisions

Even for seasoned advisors and investors, extended negative investment returns have been debilitating, and in many cases have caused them to make irrational and costly investment decisions. Had they simply examined the fundamental principles of risk, volatility, and standard deviation, and looked at what occurred in 1973-74 as being equivalent to rolling a 1 or a 6, they might have been more inclined to steadily maintain their chosen investment policy.

One of the things investors should do when looking at historical returns during down markets is to focus on the performance of asset classes when the assets rebounded. Let's take a look at what happened to the returns of large-and small-company stocks in 1975, the year following the prolonged down market of 1973 through 1974. In this year alone, the investment return of large-company stocks was a positive 37.2 percent, and small-company stocks shot up 52.8 percent. Note: when these markets rebounded, it is critical to remember that investors *had to be invested in those asset classes before the rebound* in order to participate in the positive returns. Investors who left these asset classes as a result of the chaos, pain, and confusion of 1973-1974 missed the following year's recovery.

Yet even during 1975, when the large- and small-company stocks were vigorously rebounding, Table 5-6 shows that stocks were still very volatile quarter by quarter. While the first two quarters were up strongly, a significant drop occurred in the third quarter.

Table 5-6
Quarterly Returns for Large- and Small-company Stocks in 1975

1975	Large-company Stocks	Small-company Stocks
First quarter	22.9%	51.3%
Second quarter	15.4%	18.7%
Third quarter	(11.0%)	(9.9%)
Fourth quarter	8.6%	2.4%
Yearly Return	37.2%	52.8%

If you think the rebound in 1975 seems remarkable, consider the rebound of 1933. From 1929 (at the start of the Great Depression) through 1932, the stock market collapsed. Yet in 1933, large- and small-company stocks experienced the largest single-year increase in values in history. Despite this, Table 5-7 shows that investors in these asset classes still experienced incredible quarter-by-quarter volatility, both up and down, in that unprecedented year.

Table 5-7 shows the quarterly returns for 1933, when the annual return for large-company stocks was a positive 53.9 percent and 142.9 percent for small-company stocks. As you can see, the range of returns, quarter by quarter, was enormous. Check out the return in the second quarter for small-company stocks: a mind-boggling increase of 266 percent. But then, the next two quarters provided investors with losses.

Table 5-7
Quarterly Returns for Large-and Small-company Stocks in 1933

1933	Large-company Stocks	Small-company Stocks
First quarter	(14.1%)	0.2%
Second quarter	88.8%	265.9%
Third quarter	(9.0%)	(21.8%)
Fourth quarter	4.3%	(8.9%)
Yearly Return	53.9%	142.9%

Imagine yourself as an investor in 1933. After living through four consecutive years of negative returns, you experience this incredible rebound in the first half of 1933. But before you have time to fully enjoy it, the second half of 1933 brings more investment losses. Wouldn't you be thinking "Oh no, here we go again!"

Preparing Yourself for Volatility

What would happen if the stock market went up 40 percent in any given year? This major news story would receive tremendous coverage from all levels of media—including newspapers, magazines, television, radio, and talk shows. Economists, money managers, co-workers, even your barber would have an opinion as to why the market experienced such a dramatic increase in value.

Now let's look at what would happen if the market was down 25 percent in a particular year. The coverage given to an up market would pale in comparison to the intensity of media attention that would be focused on a significant down market. The same newspapers, magazines, television, radio and talk shows would now bombard you daily with stories about the dire state of the market. It would be impossible to escape media coverage and other discussions of the down market. But the truly important question in the midst of all the hubbub is, how would you react emotionally to this?

One of the benefits of understanding historical volatility patterns is that you are likely to have more realistic expectations about the kind of market fluctuations possible in any asset class. This in turn will make you less vulnerable to reacting emotionally to the normal ups and downs that occur in the market. As we have seen, managing your *emotions* may be the most critical part of managing your *money*. This can increase your chances of staying committed to a well-conceived, long-term investment strategy.

The Crash of 1987???

Much has been written and discussed about "the Crash of 1987," when the stock market dropped more than 23 percent in a single day in October. Few people have focused on the fact that the market was actually *up 5.2 percent for the entire calendar year!* Thus, 1987 was not a down year at all; it only had a down quarter. But an investor would be hard-pressed to find a book, magazine article or newspaper story that chronicles the events of October 1987 without describing it as "the Market Crash of '87." What we never saw was a headline proclaiming *"Market Crashes in October: Still Up 5.2 Percent for Year."* The media's intense focus on reporting negative news is a useful reminder of the tremendous challenge that confronts any long-term investor.

By understanding the fundamental principles of risk and volatility, you will be better prepared to protect yourself from making unwise investment decisions in reaction to the media stories, to remain focused, and to maintain the type of discipline that is required to be a successful investor. The goal is to be able to say, in significantly up or down markets, "I guess the real news is, I simply rolled a 1 or a 6."

Personal Risk and Volatility

Other dimensions of risk should also be considered when investing. Each individual investor has a unique comfort level, or tolerance, for risk or volatility. This is not surprising, because each individual has different life experiences. One person might experience the death of a family member or go through a separation or divorce. Another person may be concerned about his own job security or that of a spouse. Both may be concerned about the stability of the industry in which they are employed. Personal factors, which we will call *personal volatility*, must be considered when investment decisions are made, since there are other dimensions of volatility that are not statistical.

Questionnaires on Risk Tolerance

More and more people today are furnished with questionnaires that attempt to quantify how much risk they can tolerate as investors. These questionnaires are designed to assist individuals to understand their comfort levels for volatility. They may also help to identify other investment objectives. The following are but a few samples of the myriad questions you might encounter in these questionnaires:

☐ In order for you to invest 10 percent of your net worth in a venture that has at least a 75 percent chance of success, the potential profit would have to be at least:

(a) the same as the amount invested

(b) three times the amount invested

(c) five times the amount invested

(d) no amount would be worth the risk

☐ Imagine you have received an inheritance or gift of $100,000. How much would you risk losing on highly volatile, risky investments?

    (a) $0

    (b) $1,000 to $15,000

    (c) $15,000 to $40,000

    (d) $40,000 to $60,000

    (e) $60,000 to $100,000

☐ Regarding your investment objectives:

    (a) you prefer to put your money in a guaranteed account where your money is absolutely safe, even if this means you will earn a lower rate of return

    (b) you prefer investments that show steady growth, but you want to beat inflation so you're willing to assume some risk

    (c) you prefer a more aggressive mix of investments, but mostly those with higher risk and the greatest chance for the highest returns

Investors must also consider personal factors and ask such questions as: How is my health or the health of other family members? How stable is my marriage or other important personal relationships? What is my job security? Will I be inheriting money? Do I have other stresses in my life? More emphasis has to be placed on such issues, which are seldom found on risk questionnaires. (This type of question cannot be asked by an employer to their employees for fear of being sued.)

The need to explore personal volatility is an excellent example of the importance of integrating not only statistical information but also behavioral information when making investment decisions. Two individuals may have the same score on their investment risk questionnaire, but because of personal factors, their actual tolerance for investment volatility can be dramatically different.

Summary: Tools for the Savvy Investor

Now that you have a better understanding of the level of risk or volatility involved in owning stocks and bonds, let's review how you can apply this information to your own investment decision making.

- By understanding the historical volatility of each of the investments you own or are considering investing in, you increase your chances of selecting or maintaining investments that reflect your personal comfort zone for risk.

- Once you understand the volatility other investors have endured to achieve higher returns, it can help you decide how to deal with the tradeoffs between the risk of inflation and the risk of volatility.

- Considering personal risk factors such as health, job security, and others will give you greater insight into the impact that personal volatility plays in the formulation of appropriate investment decisions.

- With a proper understanding of historical volatility, you may feel comfortable with taking more risk with your money, or you may discover there's too much volatility in your investments.

- By understanding the standard deviation of major asset classes, you are less likely to be surprised by normal market volatility.

- Knowing that it is "no news" for markets to be up or down in value can help you minimize emotional reactions that might trigger poor investment decisions.

- The fact that some of the best and brightest institutional investors lost their confidence in past prolonged down markets, serves as a warning to you that even the most committed individual investor may lose confidence as well.

INVESTMENT TIME HORIZONS

Some Terrible Truths

- Most people significantly underestimate how long they will be investors.

- Most investors do not recognize the inherent conflict between thinking long term and acting long term.

- One of the most well-known charts in investment education is being misinterpreted.

- An investor's rate of return may depend far more on his or her behavior than on market behavior.

- The need to make informed investment decisions does not retire when you do.

Simply stated, your investment time horizon is the length of time that your money will be invested. We tend to make investment decisions based on our perceived time horizons for specific goals such as a down payment on a house, our children's education, or accumulating the assets necessary for retirement.

Never before have so many people been required to assume the responsibility to invest their money for periods of 30 to 50 years or more. Why? The need to invest IRA, 401(k) and personal assets, in combination with dramatically increasing life expectancies, requires investors to make investment decisions for unprecedented periods of time—from today until the day they die. Most people significantly underestimate how long they will be investors. As a result, they risk running out of money during retirement or not meeting other financial goals.

Why is it essential to understand the importance of investment time horizons? Because by doing so, we can gain the information and insight necessary to choose certain types of investments over others. Understanding your true investment time horizon can also help you identify the kind of risk you are willing to take with your investments—the risk of inflation or the risk that comes with choosing more volatile investments. In addition, it can help you stay on course with specific investment strategies designed for short-, intermediate- or long-term goals. And it can help insulate you from reacting to normal market conditions or movements, either up or down.

Investment time horizons can be the most subtle and elusive of all investment principles—not because the concept is hard to grasp, but because it seems so easy. Today's investors, with unprecedented access to education and information, may *intellectually* understand "investing for the long term." But will they be able to *internalize* that understanding and put it into action over the long period of time they will be investors? There is a significant difference between *thinking* long term and truly being able to *act* long-term. History has shown that doing both—thinking long-term and acting long-term—has been incredibly difficult, and in many cases impossible, even for the most sophisticated investors.

In this Chapter...

We examine why recent research on life expectancy may significantly alter how we invest. We'll review the historical returns of various asset classes and look at their highest and lowest returns during one-, five-, ten- and twenty-year periods. This can give us valuable insight into how historical ranges of returns are impacted by time. The highest and lowest returns will then be converted into dollars to show how differing time horizons influenced them.

We will investigate why there is a major conflict between thinking and acting long-term, and how the financial media exacerbate this conflict. We will also look at what may be the most widely used chart in investment education and learn why it is misinterpreted by both investors and advisors. Finally, we will explore the role of human nature in investing, and examine the critical difference between statistical investment history and the behavioral history of investors.

Life Expectancy

As part of determining your investment time horizon, it is extremely important to look at your personal time horizon, or life expectancy. Most individuals have an unrealistic idea of how long they will live, and thus how long they will be investors. Consider the enormous implications of how long you might live. If individuals or couples live only a few years longer than they have planned for, the terrible truth is that *they may need hundreds of thousands of dollars more in order to avoid running out of money during retirement.*

Average life expectancies have almost doubled in the past 100 years. A 1995 Duke University study found that, in developed countries such as the United States, Sweden, France, England, and

Japan, a staggering 50 percent of all women and 33 percent of all men now live past the age of 80. It also concluded that men and women in the United States, once they reach the age of 80, have the longest life expectancy in the industrialized world. This study surprised many individuals who thought that people live longer in Japan and Scandinavia than they do in the U.S. In fact, the U.S. Census Bureau recently projected that 1 in 9 Baby Boomers—some 9 million persons—will live into their late 90s.

Table 6-1 contains information based on data from our government and U.S. insurance companies that estimate how long an average male and female might expect to live at various attained ages. Valuable information resides in this table. We can see what the average life expectancies are today. We can see that the older we are, the longer we can expect to live (e.g., if a female is 45, her life expectancy is 84.7; if she is 75, her life expectancy is 88.5). We can see that, on average, females outlive males. If you have purchased life insurance, you know that a male and a female of the same age are often not charged the same premium for their policies. Females have lower premiums, because the insurance company knows it will collect those premiums for a longer period of time.

Table 6-1
Individual U.S. Male and Female
Average Life Expectancies

Attained Age	Male	Female
35	79.5	84.4
40	79.8	85.5
45	80.1	84.7
50	80.6	85.0
55	81.3	85.3
60	82.1	85.8
65	83.1	86.5
70	84.5	87.4
75	86.2	88.5
80	88.5	90.1
85	91.1	92.3

Life Expectancy for Couples

So far we have considered only the life expectancy of individuals. When we consider our personal time horizons, this may not be realistic. A couple investing money for retirement cannot rely on the life expectancy of an individual.

If a couple is planning for retirement, an important question is, how long might the surviving partner be expected to live? This is called the *joint life expectancy*. Table 6-2 shows joint life expectancies for couples of the same age. (Couples who are different ages can use this table by using the age of the older of the two.) Joint life expectancy means that one or the other person in the couple will, on average, live to the age shown in the right-hand column. For the couple who are age 35, the joint life expectancy is 89; for the 50-year old couple, it is 89.3; for the 80-year old couple, it is 92.8;

and so on. When we compare the average life expectancies of couples to those of individuals, we see that the joint life expectancy is longer. This means couples will be responsible for investing their retirement assets for significantly longer periods of time than an individual and thus will also have to accumulate significantly more assets.

Table 6-2
Joint Life Expectancies of U.S. Couples

Attained Age of Couple	Joint Life Expectancy
35	89.0
40	89.1
45	89.2
50	89.3
55	89.5
60	89.7
65	90.1
70	90.7
75	91.5
80	92.8
85	94.6

People also need to be aware of recent studies conducted by life insurance companies of retired couples in excellent health—those with no major heart disease, uncontrolled high blood pressure, diabetes, cancer, or other abnormal conditions. These studies indicate that in nearly 30 percent of such cases, at least one member of the couple *will still be alive at age 95.*

The Real Rates of Return chapter included a table (Table 4-9) that shows the lump sums needed to provide an inflation-adjusted income stream ranging from 15 to 40 years in retirement at real rates of return after inflation from 1 to 8 percent. As we learn more about the latest research on longevity and life expectancies and how much longer people are living than was previously thought, it is essential to review this chart and reevaluate the number of years you might have to plan for in retirement. It will not be unusual for many investors to live 30 or 40 years in retirement.

> ### The Big Gamble — Outliving the Average
>
> As illuminating as these life expectancy tables may be, they can be extremely dangerous because they show only the *average* life expectancy of individuals and couples. Approximately 50 percent of all individuals or couples will live beyond the ages illustrated—and this does not even take into consideration the prospect of future medical breakthroughs extending life expectancies even further. Investors who base their planning on life expectancy tables are taking a tremendous risk: underestimating by just a few years how long we will live can cause many investors to run out of money in retirement.

Your Personal Genetic Profile

It is also essential to recognize the pivotal role genetics can play in life expectancy. There is overwhelming evidence that most people will live at least as long as their parents. Of course, this is subject to the influence of individual lifestyles. But your genes figure significantly in your retirement and investment decision making because they affect your investment time horizon. You must take the time to evaluate your own family history and see whether your life span is likely to exceed the average American's life expectancy. If either of your parents lived beyond the average of their generation, or if they are in excellent health, you have some crucial information that should be factored into your long-term investment planning.

It is essential that you understand current information about life expectancies, and then go through the exercise of viewing your own investment time horizon as a single period extending from today until the day you die. This exercise will give you an excellent insight into just how long you will be investors. A 50-year-old couple's average joint life expectancy is close to age 90; they will probably be investors for 40 years or more. Even if you change your investment strategy at retirement, the responsibility for managing assets continues. Remember, *the need to make informed investment decisions does not retire when you do.*

A Longer Period for Investment Time Horizons

Most of us have seen charts showing how tax-deferred savings can grow in a 401(k), IRA, or other retirement account. Such charts generally illustrate how much money might accumulate up to hypothetical retirement ages. While these charts can be helpful, they do not go nearly far enough, because some portion of the money we invest today will continue to be invested after we retire. Let's look at Chart 6-1, which illustrates how $1,000 invested at various ages today will grow to age 65, and will continue to grow from age 65 to age 85.

Chart 6-1
Pre- and Post-Retirement Growth of $1,000

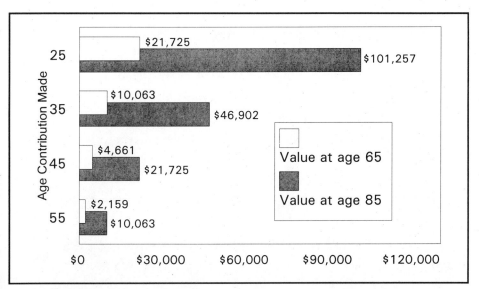

Suppose four couples, ages 25, 35, 45 and 55, make an investment of $1,000 in their retirement accounts. Assuming an 8 percent compound annual rate of return, Chart 6-1 shows how the $1,000 would accumulate for each of the four couples to both ages 65 and 85.

Let's look first at what the investment would be worth at the typical retirement age of 65, shown by the white bars. The initial $1,000 investment of the 25-year-old couple would increase over a 40-year period to $21,725. The 35-year-old couple's $1,000 investment would grow tenfold over 30 years, to $10,063. The 45-year-old couple would see their money more than quadruple to $4,661; and the 55-year-old couple would more than double their money to $2,159.

But as we've stated before, your money does not retire when you do. The gray bars in Chart 6-1 illustrate the continued growth of the investment from age 65 to age 85. From age 65 to 85, the couple who invested $1,000 at age 35 would see their money grow to $46,902, nearly 47 times their original investment. The 50-year old couple saw their $1,000 increase to $2,159 at age 65, and continue to grow to $10,063 by age 85, almost a fivefold increase in that last 20 years. Chart 6-1 reminds us of just how critical it is to recognize that you are an investor from today until death—that in almost all cases, a portion of your money will continue to grow after your retirement. Indeed, as we have already seen when reviewing current life expectancies, many investors will need their assets to grow well beyond age 85.

You Will Need All of These Assets!

It can be exciting for investors to see a portion of their assets grow from 5 to 50 times their original investment, or to see investment projections that grow into millions of dollars. But before they get too excited, they should go through the exercise of imagining themselves in retirement. After carefully taking inflation and taxes into account, most investors probably will find they'll need every one of those dollars. Perhaps Tennessee Williams's words in *Cat on a Hot Tin Roof* said it best: "You can be young without money, but you can't be old without it."

Long-term Thinking in a Short-term World

When people are asked whether they can both think and act for the long term with their investments, or whether they will abandon their well-conceived investment strategy during a prolonged down market, the overwhelming response is: "I recognize the importance of being a long-term investor, and I won't flee the market or change my long-term strategy." However, while this may seem simple, it can be a very difficult task, especially when considering the length of time you will be an investor.

Successful investing requires you to think and act for the long term, yet most areas of your personal life depend on thinking and acting for the short term. Perhaps a useful exercise would be to take a moment to sit back, reflect and observe your daily life. Most of your daily routines involve making immediate decisions and taking short-term action, from deciding what to wear to what to have for dinner. It can be critical to your health to respond quickly to toothaches or chest pains. Taking short-term action can prevent small leaks in your home from escalating to bigger ones. So, in our day-to-day lives, reacting to short-term information is a necessity.

Consider your work. Your employer gives you projects or assignments with short-term deadlines; maybe they're for one day, one month, or one year. Through personal creativity and hard work, you provide solutions, which can give you tremendous personal satisfaction. Your ability to successfully respond in the short term might also result in a bonus, a salary increase, or a job promotion. Or it might simply mean keeping your job. For most people, job performance is measured in terms of days, weeks, or months, but not decades.

In fact, the great majority of actions in our personal lives are the result of short-term decisions. So how do you separate the need to think and act for the long term in the area of investments from the necessity of thinking and acting for the short term in the other areas of your personal life? When it comes to your investment life, reacting to short-term information can be deadly. This creates a complex dilemma for individuals attempting to be long-term investors. The problem is exacerbated by the technological revolution. It has created an environment that practically invites people to make decisions based on ever-changing information and implement them by telephone, fax and the Internet faster than ever before.

The Influence of Technology

Developments in technology have transformed our lives and make us even more accustomed to short-term actions. Electronic mail, fax machines, cellular phones, computer networks and the Internet help us communicate with each other faster than ever imagined. Voice mail provides our current bank account or frequent flier mileage balance. Automated teller machines give us instantaneous access to our cash so we don't have to wait in line at the bank. News is available on television and radio every minute, 24 hours a day, 365 days a year. Sports fans no longer have to wait for the evening report to see how their favorite team fared. Through the Internet and World Wide Web, we can instantly access thousands of diverse databases of information, including medical research, adoption, libraries, genealogy, travel, restaurants, and banking.

Technology has also granted investors instant access to their investments by means of telephone, fax, or modem. Want to buy or sell stock? Go online and do it through your home computer. How has your mutual fund done in the first four hours of trading? Call the fund's automated 800 number. Investors now can make investment choices about their 401(k)s, IRAs, other retirement programs, and investment portfolios with the touch of a button.

The Conflict Presented by the Media

As if technology and other areas of our personal lives aren't enough to pressure us into taking short-term actions, let's add another ingredient: the financial media—all those investment-oriented TV and radio shows, newspapers, magazines, newsletters, and books. These sources of information also influence our thinking. The following are a few examples of headlines you may have seen in recent years:

"Market Tumble Gives Investors the Jitters"

"The Ten Best Stocks to Buy Today"

"Market Drops 170 Points on Good News of Job Growth"

"How to Double Your Money in Five Years"

"Market Overvalued; Poised for Downturn"

"Bonds Tumble on Fears of Rising Interest Rates"

"Six Warning Signs When a Market Is Ready to Plummet"

Given the length of time you will be an investor, and the probability you will experience a variety of market conditions, will it be that easy for you to ignore such overplay? After years of being bombarded with these types of headlines, stories, and news items, is it any wonder that long-term investors eventually become concerned and start questioning whether they should act *now*?

As we discussed in the chapter on Risk and Volatility, it is entirely normal for markets to fluctuate up and down. But stories in the media will not report these movements as normal; they will state that "the market soars" and "the market plummets." History has shown that the market had negative monthly returns during approximately 20 percent of the time over the past 70 years. However, you will never see a headline such as: "Market Down for Entire Month—All Is Normal."

> ## Ignoring the Conflict
>
> Given the fact that so many of our daily short-term actions produce positive results, add to this the fact that we are living in the middle of a technological and information revolution that enables us to respond to events faster than ever imagined, and then add the financial media's preoccupation with reporting short-term results. These all combine to create an atmosphere of conflict where investors' efforts to think and act for the long term can be sabotaged and fail. Yet human nature causes us to dismiss this, particularly when markets are up or our experiences with investments have been generally favorable.

Short-term History and Different Holding Periods

With a better understanding of the length of time we are going to be investors, let's revisit the history of investment returns. Earlier we looked at the rates of return of large-company stocks, small-company stocks, long-term government bonds, and Treasury bills from 1926 through 1996. It is also important to see how these asset classes performed during shorter time periods, and in particular to identify their historical best and worst rates of returns. Understanding the best and worst returns for various *holding periods* provides a valuable perspective. It illustrates what investors actually experienced for different asset classes, and it may provide information investors can use when selecting investments for different goals.

We will look at the highest and lowest returns for 1-, 5-, 10- and 20-year holding periods—periods that are probably shorter than your own investment time horizon for retirement or for other long-term financial goals. If we view ourselves as long-term investors, does it make sense to look at shorter time periods? Although it sounds paradoxical, gaining a better perspective about how asset classes have performed over the short run may give us the insight we need to be successful investors over the long run.

Table 6-3 illustrates the history of the best and worst returns over different holding periods for four asset classes from 1926 through 1996. A holding period assumes that you buy the asset class at the beginning of the first year and sell it at the end of the final year of that period. For example, the worst 5-year period for the S&P 500 stocks had a negative 12.5 percent average annual compound return, whereas the best 5-year holding period had a positive 23.9 percent average annual compound return. If we look in Table 6-3 at the 10-year holding period for Treasury bills, we see that the lowest average annual compound return was a positive 0.1 percent while the highest average annual compound return was a positive 9.2 percent.

The 1-year holding periods represent the returns for each of the 71 years from 1926 through 1996. The first 5-year holding period is from 1926 through 1930; the second from 1927 through 1931; and so on until the 67th 5-year holding period, from 1992 through 1996.

The first 10-year holding period is from 1926 through 1935; the second is from 1927 through 1936; and the 62nd is from 1987 through 1996. For the 20-year holding periods, the first is from 1926 through 1945, and the 52nd is from 1977 through 1996.

Table 6-3
Historical Returns for Different Holding Periods
(1926-1996)

Length of Holding Period	Asset Class	Lowest Average Annual Compound Return	Highest Average Annual Compound Return
1-Year	S&P 500 stocks	(43.4%)	54.0%
	Small stocks	(58.0%)	142.9%
	Long-term bonds	(9.2%)	40.4%
	Treasury bills	0.0%	14.7%
5-Years	S&P 500 stocks	(12.5%)	23.9%
	Small stocks	(27.5%)	45.9%
	Long-term bonds	(2.1%)	21.6%
	Treasury bills	0.1%	11.1%
10-Years	S&P 500 stocks	(0.9%)	20.1%
	Small stocks	(5.7%)	30.4%
	Long-term bonds	(0.1%)	15.6%
	Treasury bills	0.1%	9.2%
20-Years	S&P 500 stocks	3.1%	16.9%
	Small stocks	5.7%	21.1%
	Long-term bonds	0.7%	10.5%
	Treasury bills	0.4%	7.7%

Table 6-3 summarizes an enormous amount of data, so we will break it down by holding period using the S&P 500 stocks as our asset class example. We will look at the highest and lowest returns for 1-year, 5-year, 10-year, and 20-year holding periods, and then convert these highs and lows from each period into dollars.

Large-company U.S. Stocks:
1-Year Holding Period

There were 71 individual 1-year periods from 1926 through 1996 when an investor could have purchased large-company U.S. stocks as represented by the S&P 500 Index. Among those 71 periods, the highest single year's return showed a gain of 54.0 percent, while the lowest single year's return was a 43.3 percentage point loss. The 97.3 percentage point spread between lowest and highest returns is a graphic reminder of the volatility of equities.

1-Year Holding Period

Lowest return	(43.3%)
Highest return	54.0%
Spread	**97.3%**

5-Year Holding Period

What was the experience of investors who bought and held the S&P 500 for holding periods of 5 years? There were 68 separate 5-year holding periods from 1926 through 1996. The highest average annual compound return for the S&P 500 for a 5-year holding period was a positive 23.9 percent. The lowest 5-year period's average annual compound return was a negative compound 12.5 percent. Many investment advisors will point to these numbers as evidence that holding large-company stocks for five years instead of one year reduces the risk of potential loss for investors. The spread between the highest and lowest returns is 36.4 percentage points—some 60 percent less (viewed for a single average year of the 5-year period) than the 1-year holding-period spread.

5-Year Holding Period

Lowest return	(12.5%)
Highest return	23.9%
Spread	**36.4%**

10-Year Holding Period

There were 62 10-year holding periods from 1926 through 1996.

Looking at all the 10-year periods, we find that the highest return for large-company stocks was an average annual compound return of 20.1 percent, and the lowest return was a negative 0.9 percent—a loss of slightly less than 1 percent

10-Year Holding Period	
Lowest return	(0.9%)
Highest return	20.1%
Spread	**21.0%**

per year. We can also see that the spread between the highest and lowest returns is down to 21 percentage points.

20-Year Holding Period

Last, we can examine all 52 20-year holding periods from 1926 through 1996. The highest average annual compound return for large company stocks was 16.9 percent. Note that there were no 20-year holding periods with

20-Year Holding Period	
Lowest return	3.1%
Highest return	16.9%
Spread	**13.8%**

negative compound returns; the lowest average annual compound return was a *positive* 3.1 percent. The spread between the highest and lowest returns is now only 13.8 percentage points.

It is important to note, however, that when we look at these historical returns for the different holding periods, and determine the highest and lowest returns and the spread, we must remember that we were investing at all times in all of the stocks represented in the S&P 500 Index. Most investors did not own the entire S&P 500 during these different time periods and, as a result, their portfolios earned higher or lower returns.

Converting Percentage Returns into Dollars

We've looked at the best and worst historical returns for the S&P 500 stocks in percentages. Now let's convert these percentages into dollars, using a hypothetical $1,000 investment. This is a more graphic way to see what investors would have experienced and what they would have accumulated in an investment account for the different asset classes and holding periods illustrated in Table 6-3. In fact, any time you see data expressed in percentages, such as the track record of a mutual fund or investment manager, or other historical information, it can be an extremely helpful exercise to convert those dry percentage returns into more tangible dollars.

We saw that the lowest annual return for all 1-year holding periods was a negative 43.3 percent. The value of $1,000 invested at the beginning of that lowest year would have fallen to $557 by the end.

1-Year Holding Period	
Lowest return	$ 557
Highest return	$1,540

The highest 1-year return was a positive 54.0 percent, so the $1,000 investment would have grown in value to $1,540 by the end of that year. In other words, the outcome ranged from a loss of $433 ($1,000-557) to a gain of $540 on a $1,000 investment.

For holding periods longer than 1 year, the percentages are *compound annual returns*, which means that the returns have a cumulative effect over the entire holding period. For example, the lowest average annual compound return for a 5-year period was a negative 12.5 percent. At the end of the fifth year, you would have had

5-Year Holding Period	
Lowest return	$ 513
Highest return	$2,920

$513 in your account. The highest average annual compound return for a 5-year period was 23.9 percent. At the end of the fifth year you would have had $2,920 in your account.

For $1,000 invested in large-company stocks, the lowest 10-year compound return had an ending value of $914; the highest return had an ending value of $6,244.

10-Year Holding Period	
Lowest return	$ 914
Highest return	$6,224

Surveying all 52 of the 20-year holding periods from 1926 to 1996, we find that the period with the lowest average annual compound return had an ending value of $1,842; while the highest was $22,714. S&P 500 investors have never experienced negative returns over any 20-year period. It is important once again to emphasize that we are averaging the returns of all the stocks of the S&P 500 index. It does not show the returns that investors would have experienced by investing in other individual stocks. Many individual stocks have experienced negative returns over 20-year periods.

20-Year Holding Period	
Lowest return	$ 1,842
Highest return	$22,714

Converting Percentages into Dollars: Other Asset Classes

We have taken the S&P 500 and looked at the best and worst returns in percentages for different holding periods and then converted those percentages into dollars. Now, let's take the asset classes of small-company stocks, long-term U.S. government bonds, and Treasury bills, and go through the same exercise. Tables 6-4, 6-5 and 6-6 illustrate the lowest and highest returns as expressed in percentages for various holding periods, and then converts the percentage returns into dollars.

Table 6-4
Percentages Converted into Dollars (Impact on $1,000)
Small-company U.S. Stocks (1926-1996)

Holding Period	Lowest Return Percentage	Lowest Return Dollars	Highest Return Percentage	Highest Return Dollars
1-Year	(58.0%)	$ 420	142.9%	$ 2,429
5-Years	(27.5%)	$ 200	45.9%	$ 6,611
10-Years	(5.7%)	$ 556	30.4%	$14,216
20-Years	5.7%	$3,030	21.2%	$46,779

Table 6-5
Percentages Converted into Dollars (Impact on $1,000)
Long-term U.S. Government Bonds (1926-1996)

Holding period	Lowest Return Percentage	Lowest Return Dollars	Highest Return Percentage	Highest Return Dollars
1-Year	(9.2%)	$ 908	40.4%	$ 1,404
5-Years	(2.1%)	$ 899	21.6%	$ 2,659
10-Years	(0.01%)	$ 991	15.6%	$ 4,262
20-Years	0.7%	$1,150	10.5%	$ 7,366

Table 6-6
Percentages Converted into Dollars (Impact on $1,000)
Treasury Bills (1926-1996)

Hold Period	Lowest Return Percentage	Lowest Return Dollar	Highest Return Percentage	Highest Return Dollars
1-Year	0.0%	$ 1,000	14.7%	$ 1,147
5-Years	0.1%	$ 1,005	11.1%	$ 1,693
10-Years	0.2%	$ 1,010	9.2%	$ 2,411
20-Years	0.4%	$ 1,083	7.7%	$ 4,409

Summary of Holding Periods

A historical review of best and worst returns for different holding periods in terms of dollars rather than percentages offers enormous insight for investors in the selection of investments. By reviewing this information, investors may have more realistic expectations about what could result from their investment choices. Potential account values can give investors a perspective that percentages simply cannot provide.

For example, we know that at the end of the worst 10-year period for the S&P 500—a period that included the Great Depression—investors in this asset class still had more than 90 cents on the dollar left in their accounts. Some observers will say, "Look at that—after holding onto investments for a full decade, they still lost money." Such observers might view large-company stocks as risky.

But others might come to the conclusion that, if history's worst 10-year investment period preserved more than 90 cents on the dollar, there is every reason to feel optimistic and encouraged about the strategy of remaining a long-term investor in this asset class.

Either way, investors are well served, because this dollar-based analysis can increase their chances of selecting investments suited to their investment time horizons, their emotions, or both.

This is very important since many investors are not risk averse; they are *loss averse*. That is, they feel comfortable taking the risk of attempting to get higher returns so long as they never see their money decrease in value. Those investors in particular should study historical holding periods to see what the potential for loss could be. When investors review the best and worst historical returns of various asset classes in dollars, they gain added insights that enhance the likelihood they will make better long-term decisions. They also may reduce their chances of letting their emotions get in the way of good investment decision-making.

Stocks Versus "Risk-free" Investments

When people invest in stocks, they have chosen a relatively volatile investment. As we discussed in the Volatility chapter, history has shown that the stock market has gone through numerous periods of time when stocks have significantly declined in value. When this happens, it is human nature for investors to wish that their money was in risk-free investments, insulated from plummeting stock prices. However, would investors have been better off with risk-free investments? Let's turn back the clock and run a hypothetical investment race.

Suppose that one investor put $10,000 in the S&P 500 during the worst-performing 1-, 10-, and 20-year holding periods. Another investor put $10,000 in risk-free Treasury bills during the same periods of time. Let's follow this investment race and see what would have happened. Table 6-7 compares the worst performing 1-, 10-, and 20-year returns for large-company U.S. stocks with the returns for T-bills during these same periods. Look at the worst-performing

1-year holding period, and you can see that the value of $10,000 invested in the S&P 500 dropped to $5,670 by the end of that year, while at the end of the same 1-year holding period the T-bills were worth $10,110.

Table 6-7
Large-company Stocks versus Treasury Bills

Worst Holding Period for Large-company Stocks	Value of $10,000 Stock Investment	Treasury Bill Value During Same Period
1-Year	$ 5,670	$10,110
10-Years	$ 9,140	$11,070
20-Years	$18,420	$11,410

But as the holding period grows, we can see the trend begin to reverse. At the end of the worst 10-year period for large-company stocks, the spread between the returns has narrowed to less than $2,000. If you knew that at the end of the worst 10-year period historically for large-company stocks you would still have $9,140 left of your original $10,000, would this influence your investment choice?

Now let's look at the worst 20-year holding period. You can see that large-company stocks significantly outperformed T-bill investing—$18,420 compared to $11,410 in our hypothetical race, or more than 61 percent more money.

NOTE: *These figures assume the full reinvestment of dividends, no income taxes, and no transaction costs.*

The use of such tables and statistics has traditionally encouraged people to invest in stocks. But remember, they really only tell part of the story. What is not illustrated is the enormous volatility that an investor would have endured throughout this 20-year period. Chart

6-2 illustrates this on a month-to-month basis. After seeing this, is it still clear that an investor could stay 100% invested in stocks over a long period of time?

Chart 6-2
Monthly Returns of Large-company U.S. Stocks
Worst 20-Year Period

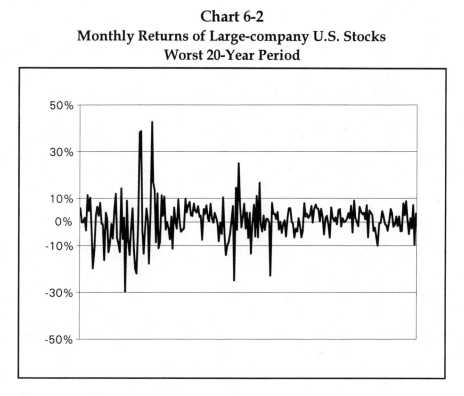

Misinterpreting Data: Does Time Always Reduce Risk?

Many financial books, magazines, newspapers, educational and promotional materials use statistical graphs and charts to illustrate or explain particular points. It is easy to look at these, nod your head, and accept the information without further thought or examination. Yet even though the data contained in these charts may be accurate, relying on their conclusions at face value could cause you to make critical investment decisions based on incomplete information.

Statistics — Dangerous if Viewed in Isolation

Let's assume than an investor could have endured the enormous market volatility of the S&P 500 throughout a given 20-year period. However, what if during the same period of time this investor had experienced the type of personal volatility that we have discussed throughout this book? Job loss, domestic strife or other personal difficulties could impact the investor's ability to stay committed to the stock market throughout the 20 years. Only by considering personal volatility along with market volatility can we get a clearer picture of the challenges that this hypothetical investor would have to confront to finish the race and collect the extra return offered by stocks over the risk-free return. This is yet another reminder that we must be careful when looking at historical investment returns not to ignore behavioral considerations.

Chart 6-3 presents a well-known graph that is used extensively by some of the nation's most respected financial writers, advisors, and educators, as well as established publications and institutions. It serves to illustrate how an accurate graph can be unwittingly misinterpreted. This graph is used to show that the longer you hold an investment in stocks, the lower your risk in owning them. In other words, the message conveyed is that the risk of holding stocks was reduced over time. It tracks the best and worst performances of the S&P 500 for 1-, 5-, 10 and 20-year holding periods over 71 years. When we carefully examine the graph step by step and then convert the results into dollars, we discover just how easily we can misinterpret not only this graph, but other investment charts and graphs as well.

Chart 6-3
How Holding Periods Affect Best and Worst Returns
of S&P 500 (1926-1996)

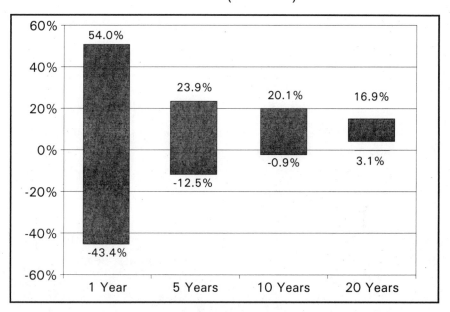

The bar on the extreme left of the graph shows that, in the best 1-year holding period for the S&P 500 since 1926, investors would have earned a 54 percent gain, while they would have lost 43 percent of their money in the worst 1-year period. During the best 5-year period, an investment in the S&P 500 would have increased in value by an average annual compound return of 23.9 percent. It would have decreased by an annual compound rate of 12.5 percent during the worst 5-year period. For the 10-year periods, the best performance was a compound annual gain of 20.1 percent, and the worst performance was a compound annual 0.9 percent loss. Finally, the best average annual compound return over a 20-year holding period was a positive 16.9 percent, and the worst was a positive 3.1 percent.

So far, the graph in Chart 6-3 appears to confirm that as holding periods get longer, the risk of investing in these stocks is reduced. The worst 1-year period showed a 43 percent loss; the worst 5-year period showed a 12.5 percent compound loss; the worst 10-year period produced a 0.9 percent compound loss; and the worst 20-year period showed a 3.1 percent compound gain. The losses get progressively smaller over time and eventually end in a gain for the longest holding period—all of which appears to confirm that the longer the holding period, the smaller the risk.

Investors generally are reassured by this graph. They look at it and incorrectly conclude that, at the end of the all-time worst 5-year period, they still would have close to 90 percent of their money left. As a result, many investors are led to feel that if they can hold their stocks for 5 years, even in a worst-case scenario they would incur a very limited amount of loss.

Chart 6-4 illustrates the worst performing 1-and 5-year holding periods in percentages for the S&P 500. It shows that the worst-performing 5-year period had a substantially smaller negative return than the worst performing one-year period.

Chart 6-4
Holding Periods in Percentages
Worst Return for One and Five Years

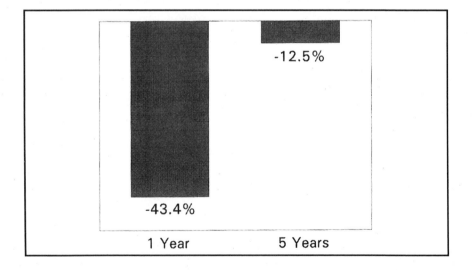

-12.5%

-43.4%

1 Year   5 Years

But as an investor, you do not invest in *percentages*, you invest your hard-earned *dollars*. Chart 6-5 shows what happens when we convert the percentages into dollars. We find that a $1,000 investment would have declined in value to $567 in the worst 1-year period. At the end of the worst 5-year period, *the same $1,000 would have declined to $513.*

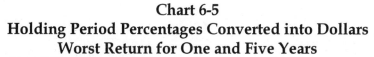

Chart 6-5
Holding Period Percentages Converted into Dollars
Worst Return for One and Five Years

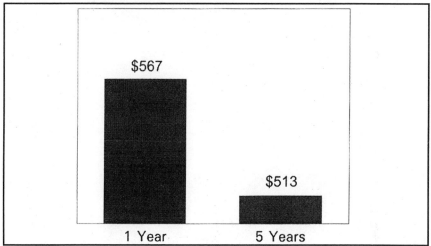

$567	
	$513
1 Year	5 Years

Investors who thought that the negative 12.5 percent rate of return represented the total percentage drop over the entire worst 5-year period would conclude that 87.5 percent of their initial $1,000 would still be available at the end of that period (100%-12.5%). But this is simply not the case. In reality, *an investor would actually have fewer dollars at the end of the worst five-year period than at the end of the single worst year in stock market history.*

Why have so many people erroneously concluded from Chart 6-3 that the worst 5-year holding period was less risky than the worst 1-year period? The answer is that the negative 12.5 percent return for the worst 5-year holding period is *compounded for each year* of the 5-year holding period. If you invested $1,000 at the beginning of the first year and received a negative 12.5 percent return, you would lose $125 and have $875 at the end of the first year. *But if you continued to lose 12.5 percent each year for the next four years, at the end of the fifth year you would end up with only $513—not $875.*

Table 6-8
5 Years of Negative 12.5 Percent Annual Compound Return

Year	Return	Ending Value of $1,000
1	(12.5%)	$875
2	(12.5%)	$766
3	(12.5%)	$700
4	(12.5%)	$586
5	(12.5%)	$513

Misleading Charts and Statistics

Countless financial articles have recommended that if investors have a 5-year period to invest, it is a long enough period to confidently invest in equities. These recommendations are based on the perception that if the worst 1-year period produced a negative 43 percent and the worst 5-year period produced only a negative 12.5 percent, investors reduced their risk with a longer holding period. But investors who base investment decisions on data that is misleading can find themselves making investment decisions that are inconsistent with their true investment time horizon. Investors need to convert percentages into dollars in order to reveal the true performance.

Does risk ever go away? Investors should never forget that however long the holding period or time horizon of their investments may be, equities will always be subject to market volatility on a day-to-day, month-to-month, and year-to-year basis—no different than the personal volatility we encounter as a part of our everyday lives. The moment you invest a dollar in volatile investments, there is no guarantee you will not lose some or all of that dollar, no matter how long you hold the investment. If there truly was such a guarantee, risk would simply not exist.

Summary: Tools for the Savvy Investor

What have we gained by better understanding the relationship between our personal time horizon and our investments' time horizons?

- By reviewing current life expectancy tables and studies on longevity, we know that Americans are living longer than ever before. This understanding helps you avoid underestimating the time you will be an investor.

- Your investment time horizon extends from today until the day you die. Understanding the true length of time you will be responsible for investing your assets increases your chances of choosing appropriate investments.

- Much of the investment data and information we receive is misinterpreted. One way to counteract this is to convert percentage investment returns into dollars. This gives you a clearer picture of potential investment results.

- The inherent struggle between thinking long term and acting short term is easily dismissed by investors. Being aware of this conflict reduces your chances of overreacting to market fluctuations.

- History has shown that when investing in stocks, the longer the holding period the smaller the chance of losing money. But you should never lose sight of the fact that this risk of loss can never be entirely eliminated.

DIVERSIFICATION

Some Terrible Truths

- Many investors believe they have well-diversified portfolios when in fact they do not.

- Without proper diversification, some investors may be taking more risk than necessary with their investments.

- Some investors who diversify actually increase volatility in their portfolios without realizing it.

- Investors can achieve the goal of reducing risk with diversification, yet still be disappointed by their portfolio's returns.

- No matter how well a portfolio is diversified, investors must always deal with nondiversifiable risk.

- Diversification neither guarantees successful investment performance nor eliminates losses from a portfolio.

- Investors do not understand what they have to give up in order to receive the benefits of diversification.

Almost all investors are familiar with the term *diversification*. Put most simply, diversification follows the adage: "Don't put all your eggs in one basket." But diversification is more complex than this. In fact, Harry M. Markowitz, a professor at the University of Chicago, won a Nobel prize in economics primarily for his work in this area.

Why do investors diversify? Some do it in hopes of reducing the overall volatility in their portfolios. Others diversify so they can get higher returns, necessary to attain long-term financial goals.

Experts uniformly agree that diversification is a necessary element in investing. However, asking ten financial experts how they diversify their client's portfolios is like asking ten economists a question: you might get fifteen different answers.

In This Chapter...

Because experts can't agree on a common interpretation of diversification, let's try to understand it by looking at a number of examples. We will start with that of owning a single stock versus owning a group of stocks, and review some potential outcomes. In doing so we will look at the advantages of diversifying and, just as important, explore what investors must give up when they diversify. Using this as our starting point, we will see how diversification applies to other investments as well.

We will then see why, by investing in two asset classes instead of one, a hypothetical investor would experience less volatility in his portfolio over the long term due to the benefits of *cross-correlation*. We will examine the potential advantages to be gained by combining several different asset classes in a portfolio such as stocks, bonds, international securities, and money market funds. Finally, using a series of scenarios we will look at how diversification, despite all of its benefits, can still cause confusion and disillusionment if investors don't understand its advantages and disadvantages in advance.

Buying a Single Stock Versus a Group of Stocks

Let's look at two hypothetical investments of $10,000 as we begin to study diversification. One investor puts $10,000 in a single corporation, the Acme Company, which is listed on the New York Stock Exchange with a current market value of $50 a share. The second investor puts the $10,000 in 10 companies which are listed on the New York stock exchange, one of which is Acme. These companies represent different industries such as manufacturing, retail, electronics, and transportation. (The same comparison could be made when buying a single bond versus a group of them or buying single versus multiple investments in other asset classes.) Let's examine some potential outcomes of purchasing stock exclusively in Acme Company versus buying the group of stocks that includes Acme.

Potential for Total Loss

First of all, by owning only one stock, you risk losing the entire value of your investment. If Acme goes into bankruptcy or goes completely out of business, its stock usually becomes worthless. But if you own a group of companies, you greatly reduce the chance your entire investment will be lost, because it is less likely all the companies will go bankrupt at the same time. This is called "diversifiable risk."

Potential for Higher Return

On the other hand, by investing the entire $10,000 in Acme, an investor has the opportunity to obtain a significantly higher rate of return than if he had bought the group of stocks. The return for the second investor who buys the group of stocks will be the average of the returns of all of the stocks in the group. This average may turn out to be lower than Acme's return. For example, if Acme's stock increases in value from $50 per share to $75 per share, the first investor will enjoy a 50 percent return (illustrated in Chart 7-1). Meanwhile, the second investor who chose to diversify may earn an average return of 15 percent.

Chart 7-1
Potential for Higher Return

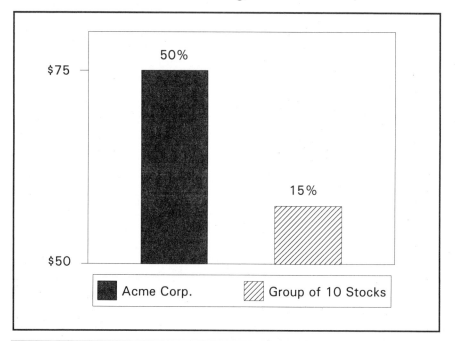

Second Guessing

In our example, Acme went up 50 percent, while the average of the group of 10 stocks increased only 15 percent. Wouldn't it be natural for you to feel "I should have put more money in Acme, maybe even all of it?" Human nature can cause anyone to second-guess investment decisions. Ironically, this problem is only going to increase along with the number of choices investors are given to diversify their portfolios.

Potential for Lower Return

It is also possible that Acme's return could turn out to be lower than the average of the group. Picture Acme not competing successfully within its industry and suffering substantial financial hardship, causing its stock to tumble from $50 per share to $20 per share—an 80 percent loss in value (as shown in Chart 7-2). It is highly unlikely that all the companies in the group would suffer the same level of financial hardship experienced by Acme. In our example, the average return for the entire group of stocks declines by 20 percent.

Chart 7-2
Potential for Lower Return

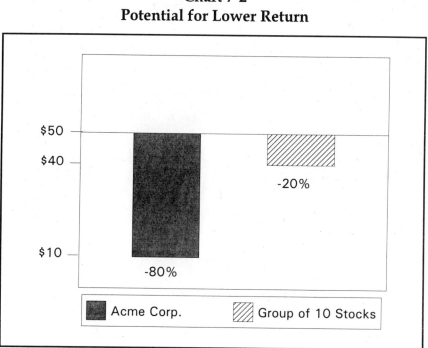

Same Average Return but Higher Volatility

Owning Acme or any other single stock rather than a group of stocks might result in the same average return over a long period of time but an investor could experience higher volatility with an individual stock. Suppose that over the past decade Acme's returns averaged 10 percent and so did the group of stocks. During this decade, however, Acme's stock experienced volatile price swings both up and down, as shown by the narrow line in Chart 7-3.

Now let's compare Acme's volatility with the volatility of the group of stocks. Because each stock in the group had its own different pattern of return, the average volatility of the group was significantly lower than Acme's, as illustrated by the thick line in Chart 7-3. Although Acme and the group of 10 stocks had the same 10 percent average return, an investor in the group of stocks would have experienced significantly less volatility from year to year.

Chart 7-3
Lower Volatility of Group

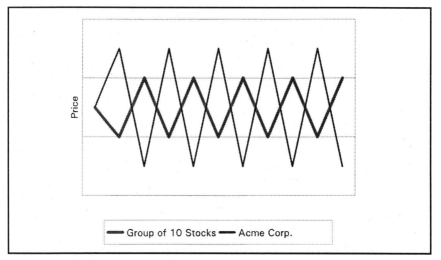

Different Approaches to Diversification

Diversification can take on many different appearances. For some investors, it may mean buying stock in 10 companies as opposed to one; others may want to invest in 50 companies instead of three. Diversifying could mean buying stocks in several companies within the same industry (e.g., buying Chrysler, Ford, General Motors, and Toyota); or it could mean deciding to buy stock of companies in different industries, such as pharmaceutical, banking, and utilities. Diversification can also include investing in different asset classes, such as stocks, bonds, and money market funds, considering both U.S. and international investments.

Just one reason for the phenomenal growth in the mutual fund industry has been a growing recognition by investors of the benefits of diversification. By the middle of 1997 more than $4.0 trillion was invested in over 8,000 mutual funds. Mutual funds provide investors with the opportunity to invest and diversify in a broad variety of asset classes, from domestic and international stocks and bonds to real estate.

Advantages and Disadvantages of Diversifying

So far we have seen some of the advantages of diversification across a group of stocks as compared to owning a single stock. These include reduced portfolio volatility, reduced potential for significant loss in value, and reduced risk of complete forfeiture of an investment.

Before we move on, let's review what you may be giving up if you choose to diversify your portfolio. You may give up not only the opportunity and enjoyment of getting higher returns, but also the dream of hitting an investment "home run." Is this something you are willing to forfeit? Decisions about whether, when, and how to diversify can be made only by each investor or advisor based on individual facts and circumstances.

> ## Nondiversifiable Risk Never Goes Away
>
> Investors, particularly those whose investment experiences have been favorable, need to constantly remind themselves that, no matter how well they are diversified, they are always at risk of suffering a loss or seeing their assets decline in value due to general market conditions. This risk is called *market risk* or *nondiversifiable risk*. The uncertainty and unpredictability of markets can never be completely diversified away.

Diversifying with More than One Asset Class

Many investors attempt to diversify further by investing in more than one asset class, such as bonds, money market accounts, real estate, and international stocks.

To begin to understand the impact of this level of diversification, let's create a portfolio that includes just two asset classes—the S&P 500 and long-term U.S. government bonds. We will assume that this portfolio is invested 50 percent in the S&P 500 Index and 50 percent in 20-year government bonds, for the 30-year period of 1967 through 1996. From the Volatility chapter we know that historically, the S&P 500 had more volatility than long-term government bonds, and that it also earned higher returns for investors.

First we will look at the average return of each of these two asset classes over the 30-year period in question; then we will look at portfolio return when they are combined. Next we will examine the individual volatility (standard deviation) of these two asset classes over the same period, and see what happens to portfolio volatility when the two classes are combined.

Table 7-1 shows the average annual compound return for the S&P 500 and long-term U.S. government bonds from 1967 through 1996.

Table 7-1
Average Annual Compound Return (1967-1996)

	S&P 500	Long-term Govt. Bonds
Compound Return	12%	8%

Note: Numbers rounded

Let's see what the average return would be for our hypothetical portfolio of 50 percent S&P 500 stocks and 50 percent long-term bonds over this period. Since the S&P 500's returns were 12 percent and the bonds' returns were 8 percent over this period, we would expect a 50/50 portfolio to yield a return that combines half of 12 percent and half of 8 percent, or 10 percent. Table 7-2 confirms what we expected—the combined portfolio's average return was indeed 10 percent over this 30-year period.

Table 7-2
Portfolio Average Compound Return (1967-1996)

Asset Class	Compound Return	Percent of Portfolio	Contribution to Portfolio
S&P 500	12%	x 50%	6%
Long-term Bonds	8%	x 50%	4%
TOTAL		100%	10%

Note: Numbers rounded

Now, let's perform a similar calculation to average the standard deviations of the S&P 500 and long-term government bonds over this same 30-year period. As we discussed in the Volatility chapter, standard deviation is a measurement of volatility—and thus of risk. The higher the standard deviation, the higher the risk. The standard deviation for the S&P 500 for this period was 16 percent, while the standard deviation of long-term government bonds was 12 percent. Let's average these two numbers just as we averaged the returns. As Table 7-3 indicates, the resulting average standard deviation is 14 percent.

Table 7-3
Average Portfolio Volatility (1967–1996)

Asset Class	Standard Deviation	Percent of Portfolio	Contribution to Portfolio Deviation
S&P 500	16%	x 50%	8.0%
Long-term Bonds	12%	x 50%	6.0%
TOTAL		100%	14.0%

Note: Numbers rounded

However, the actual historic standard deviation of this 50/50 portfolio was not 14 percent as one might expect, but 12 percent. Why did investors experience lower volatility than expected when these two asset classes were combined? Because of the effects of cross-correlation.

Cross-correlation

The reason the 50/50 portfolio had a lower standard deviation than a simple averaging of the standard deviations over the 30-year period is that the return of the stocks and the bonds fluctuated up and down, but not necessarily at the same time. In some years, stocks were up in value when bonds were down, and vice versa. As a result of these dissimilar patterns of returns, when we combined the asset classes into our 50/50 portfolio, the overall volatility was reduced. This beneficial effect, called *cross-correlation*, was identified in Nobel prize–winning research by Harry M. Markowitz and is part of "Modern Portfolio Theory."

In our example, the overall volatility of the portfolio was less than the simple average volatility of the two asset classes. In fact, this portfolio actually had less overall volatility than a portfolio invested 100 percent in long-term government bonds for the same time period! This is illustrated in Chart 7-4 on the following page.

Chart 7-4
Standard Deviations of S&P 500,
Long-term Government Bonds,
and a 50/50 Portfolio of the Two
(1967-1996)

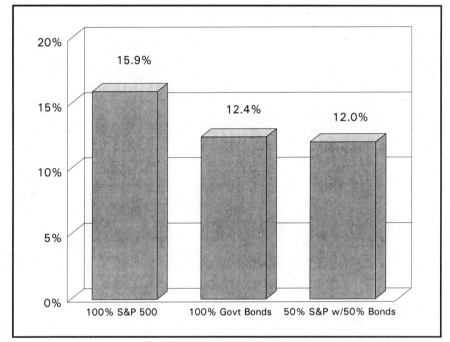

To see why volatility was reduced in the combined portfolio, let's examine Table 7-4, which illustrates the year-by-year performance of these two asset classes for the 30-year period of 1967-1996. Years in which one asset class had a positive return while the other asset class had a negative return are shaded. As the table shows, this occurred 11 times during the 30-year period.

Table 7-4
Annual Returns of S&P 500 and Long-term
Government Bonds (1967-1996)

Year	S&P 500	Long-term Govt. Bonds
1967	24.0%	(9.2%)
1968	11.1%	(0.3%)
1969	(8.5%)	(5.1%)
1970	4.0%	12.1%
1971	14.3%	13.2%
1972	19.0%	5.7%
1973	(14.7%)	(1.1%)
1974	(26.5%)	4.4%
1975	37.2%	9.2%
1976	23.8%	16.8%
1977	(7.2%)	(0.7%)
1978	6.6%	(1.2%)
1979	18.4%	(1.2%)
1980	32.4%	(4.0%)
1981	(4.9%)	1.9%
1982	21.4%	40.4%
1983	22.5%	0.7%
1984	6.3%	15.5%
1985	32.2%	31.0%
1986	18.5%	24.5%
1987	5.2%	(2.7%)
1988	16.8%	9.7%
1989	31.5%	18.1%
1990	(3.2%)	6.2%
1991	30.5%	19.3%
1992	7.7%	9.4%
1993	10.0%	18.2%
1994	1.3%	(7.8%)
1995	37.4%	31.7%
1996	23.1%	(0.9)%

Parentheses indicate negative returns.

Cross-correlation—Beneficial Even While Losing

Even in years when investments decline in value, it is still possible to benefit from cross-correlation and achieve reduction in a portfolio's volatility. For example, Table 7-4 indicates that in 1973 the S&P 500 was down 14.7 percent while long-term government bonds were down 1.1 percent. But even though both these asset classes had negative returns, our hypothetical 50/50 portfolio had less volatility than an all-stock portfolio. Although an investor's reaction to a year that produced negative returns in both asset classes may have been disappointment, the important goal of reducing volatility was still achieved.

Another way to understand cross-correlation is to look at Chart 7-5 where two investments go up and down in value. This chart gives us a chance to see what numbers alone cannot illustrate. The dotted line, shows the pattern of volatility of "asset class A"over time; the dashed line represents "asset class B." The solid line AB illustrates how volatility is smoothed out when these two asset classes are combined 50/50 in a portfolio.

Chart 7-5
Cross-correlation of Two Asset Classes

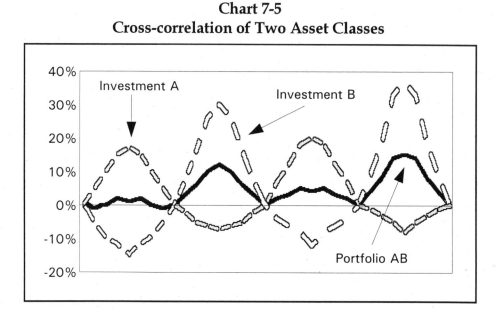

Diversification With Various Asset Classes

Many different asset classes can be used to diversify a portfolio. The following is just a partial list.

- Cash and cash equivalents—Treasury bills, money market funds, CDs

- Domestic government or corporate bonds
    Short term (one to two years in maturity)
    Intermediate term (two to ten years maturity)
    Long term (over ten years in maturity)

- International bonds—bonds issued by governments or corporations outside the United States

- U.S. stocks—typically divided into groups based on the market value of the company
  Large-company stock
  Midsized-company stocks
  Small-company stocks

- International stocks—stocks in corporations located outside the U.S.
  Large-company stocks
  Midsized-company stocks
  Small-company stocks

- Emerging markets—stocks in corporations located in less-developed countries or newer stock markets

- Real estate

- Gold, silver and other precious metals

- Commodities

Of course, each of these asset classes contains many investment choices.

When we consider diversifying with different asset classes, we need to remember the example of what occurs when investing in one stock versus a group of stocks and consider the potential outcomes. Should an investor limit his or her portfolio to one asset class as opposed to a group of them? Each asset class has its own separate pattern of return.

The graphs shown in Chart 7-6 plot the returns of some major asset classes from 1970 to 1996. We can see how each of these asset classes had a different pattern of return. Thus, if an investor combines asset classes that have dissimilar patterns of returns, the overall volatility of the portfolio may be reduced.

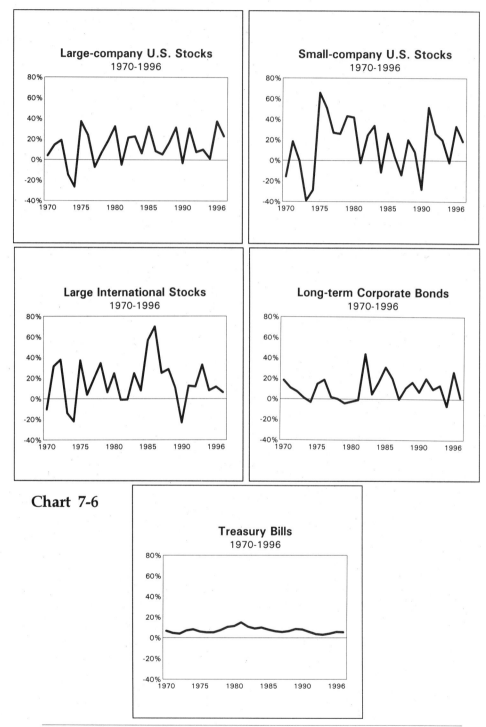

Chart 7-6

Diversification with International Investments

The world's investment picture has radically changed over the past 25 years, and the U.S. no longer dominates the global economy to the extent it once did. The following pie chart (Chart 7-7) illustrates the proportion of money invested in the U.S. stock market and non-U.S. stock markets. They clearly show that there has been a shift in the world's stock markets away from a majority of money invested in the U.S. to a majority invested outside the U.S. In 1970 the U.S. stock market represented more than two-thirds of the value of the world's equity markets; but 27 years later this figure dropped to approximately 40 percent.

Chart 7-7
World's Equity Markets Divided by U.S. and Non-U.S.

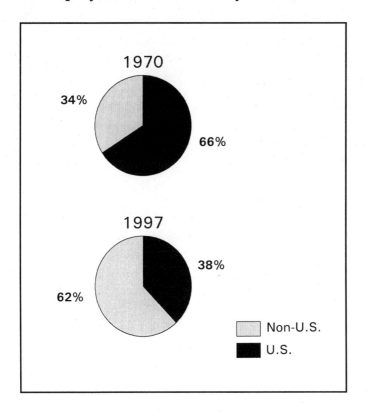

Today many investors consider diversifying their portfolios by investing outside of the United States. Many mutual funds already hold international investments and numerous large institutional pension plans include international stocks and bonds as a part of their portfolios. The number of mutual funds that offer investors the choice of investing internationally has increased significantly, and more and more 401(k) plans are including international investment options. For example, in 1987 only 81 mutual funds offered investments in international markets. Just $17 billion was invested in these funds. Today more than $300 billion is invested in over 650 mutual funds investing in international markets.

This major shift toward international investing may have been originally sparked by U.S. investors who saw how international markets outperformed U.S. markets in many years. That, in conjunction with the increasing desire of some investors to further diversify portfolios or to invest in emerging markets such as those in Southeast Asia, Latin America and Eastern Europe helps explain this enormous growth.

Investment experts express various opinions about the advantages and disadvantages of international investing and the role it should play in diversification. Many investors own stocks in U.S. companies that generate a major part of their business and revenues outside of the U.S. and count that as international diversification. How those stocks should be viewed in comparison with investing internationally remains subject to debate. As with any other asset class, investors and their advisors need to evaluate individually how and whether international investments should be included in their overall portfolio design.

> ## International Investing
>
> Some of you may already be international investors and not be aware of it. Many mutual funds already have 10 to 20 percent or more of their portfolio invested internationally. Some funds or investment advisors invest 50 percent of their assets internationally. Consequently, investors should check to see what percent of their portfolios have already been committed to international markets.

Other Possible Benefits

Diversification has other potential benefits as well. In some cases, if diversification reduces volatility in a portfolio, the actual growth of dollars in the portfolio increases, as taught to me by Roger C. Gibson, CFA, of Gibson Capital Management in Pittsburgh, PA. This situation is illustrated in the following example.

Suppose we have two portfolios, one of which is diversified while the other is not. Portfolio A, not diversified, earns 16 percent in the first year, loses 8 percent in the second year, and earns 16 percent in the third year. Let's compare this with the diversified Portfolio B, which earns 8 percent in Year One, Year Two and Year Three.

Both of these hypothetical portfolios have the same average return—8 percent. But let's examine what happens if we start with $10,000 and follow its growth in value to the end of the third year. Under these conditions, Portfolio A would be worth $12,380 at the end of three years and Portfolio B would grow to $12,597. *Even when two portfolios have the same average returns, the one with lower volatility will accumulate more money.* And, not only is there more money in Portfolio B; just as important, because the investor in this portfolio experienced lower volatility, he may be more inclined to stay committed to his long-term investment strategy.

Table 7-5
Comparing Returns of Non-diversified and
Diversified Portfolios

	Year One	Year Two	Year Three	Growth of $10,000
Portfolio A (Non-diversified)	16%	(8%)	16%	$12,380
Portfolio B (Diversified)	8%	8%	8%	$12,597

Diversification—Caveats and Concerns

Diversification is a widely accepted investment principle and can offer investors significant benefits. Too often, however, these benefits are oversimplified and even misinterpreted. It can be dangerous for investors to believe that diversification guarantees them investment success or protects them from all investment losses. Let's look at five scenarios to help investors avoid the disillusionment, disappointment and confusion that can come with diversifying their portfolios.

Scenario One

An investor's portfolio consists of five different investments. His objective is to reduce volatility, so he has included a variety of asset classes that have a history of dissimilar patterns of return. At the end of the first year he sees that four of the five investments increased in value while one went down by 15 percent. Even though the portfolio as a whole had a positive return, the investor seems able to focus only on the investment that lost 15 percent. As a result, he is frustrated and disappointed with his portfolio's overall performance.

The irony is that his investment objective of diversifying the portfolio to reduce volatility was actually achieved. But the investor's reaction to the loss in value of just one investment has caused him to lose sight of why he diversified his portfolio in the first place. This emotional response demonstrates why financial advisors say: "Investors are not risk averse, they are *loss averse.*"

Scenario Two

An investor has a diversified portfolio that contains eight different types of asset classes, including U.S. and international stocks. The portfolio's investments range from higher-risk international small-company stocks to lower-risk U.S. Treasury bills. Because the investor feels his portfolio is well diversified, he is confident about the portfolio's ability not only to minimize volatility but also to achieve satisfactory long-term investment performance.

But suppose that four of his investments go up in value and four go down, and the overall portfolio value declines by 15 percent. The investor protests, "Wait a minute! This wasn't supposed to happen, I'm too well diversified." In his emotional response to seeing his portfolio decline in value, he forgot that his portfolio contains a number of higher-risk, higher-potential-return investments that always have the potential to go down significantly in value. This can be particularly hard on an investor who has never before experienced a substantial investment loss.

Scenario Three

An employee owns ten different mutual funds in his 401(k) plan. From the names and descriptions of these funds in their prospectuses, the investor believes his portfolio is well diversified. But after carefully analyzing the funds' investments, he discovers that he is actually not very well diversified: nine of the ten mutual funds are invested in the same asset class. Thus, this investor's portfolio has little chance of achieving its original investment objective—a diversified portfolio that attempts to reduce volatility by holding different asset classes with dissimilar patterns of return.

The same problem can affect an investor who buys a group of individual stocks. In his enthusiasm for the stocks he has selected for his portfolio, he may overlook the fact that they all fall into the same industry or segment of the market.

Scenario Four

An investor who has previously owned only money market funds, certificates of deposit and Treasury bills now adds stocks and bonds to his portfolio in hope of achieving higher rates of return. The investor recognizes that the new portfolio is better diversified than the old one, and everything he has read or been told assures him that increased diversification is always beneficial. However, the investor needs to be aware that, when he moves from his low-risk, all cash-equivalent type of portfolio to a more diversified one in the attempt to get higher returns, he receives a guarantee—*that the new portfolio will have higher risk and greater volatility.* Unless the investor understands this and is prepared in advance for greater volatility, adverse returns at any point could make him vulnerable to reacting with panic and confusion. As a result, he could end up moving away from a portfolio design that was appropriate for him over the long term.

Scenario Five

At the end of 1994 an investor had 70 percent of his portfolio in U.S. large-company stocks, 25 percent in bonds, and 5 percent in cash equivalents. With a desire to earn higher returns and to further diversify the stock portion of his portfolio, he added small-company U.S. stocks and large-company international stocks, reducing the percentage of his portfolio that was previously allocated to large-company U.S. stocks. During the next three years, 1995 through 1997, the investor saw his large-company U.S. stocks go up by more than 60 percent in value while his small-company U.S. and international stocks increased by 10 percent in value. As a result, he is frustrated: he feels he should not have diversified and should have stayed with large-company U.S. stocks because that would have produced significantly higher returns.

Investors who choose to diversify by adding other asset classes with the objective of earning higher returns should, in advance, consider the following:

1. In the short and long term, an investor's objective of higher returns may not be met;

2. The overall rate of return of a diversified portfolio will always be lower than the rate of return of the highest-performing investment in the portfolio; and

3. Investors should not second-guess investment decisions. Hindsight yields scant benefits for future planning.

Diversification: Final Observations

Diversification's ability to reduce risk or volatility in a portfolio and its potential for helping investors achieve important investment goals and objectives should not be overlooked by any investor. However, no matter how well a portfolio is diversified, it may still carry more risk than a particular investor can tolerate. Investors must keep in mind that diversification neither guarantees them positive investment performance, nor completely protects them from investment losses.

When you diversify, it is important to go through the exercise of examining the historical volatility and risk characteristics of each and every asset class you consider adding to your portfolio. A thorough understanding of each investment in a portfolio significantly reduces the chance that you will overreact to the normal ups and downs of a particular investment.

Summary: Tools for the Savvy Investor

Now that we're equipped with a better understanding of diversification and cross-correlation, let's review how you can apply this information to investment decision making.

- Regardless of how well your portfolio is diversified, you cannot completely eliminate risk. There is always nondiversifiable risk—the risk that comes from the uncertainty and unpredictability of the market itself.

- Understanding both the advantages and disadvantages of diversification can increase your chances of remaining committed to a diversified portfolio over the long term.

- Historically, diversification has provided the opportunity to lower the risk or the volatility of portfolios without necessarily sacrificing returns.

- Even though two investment portfolios may have the same average return, the one with lower volatility will accumulate more money over time.

- Even in years when your investments have declined in value, you can still benefit from diversification and reduce the volatility of your portfolio.

- Taking advantage of cross-correlation can reduce a portfolio's risk and volatility. Such a reduction in volatility may be the only way for you to weather declining markets.

- You may believe you have a well-diversified portfolio but upon more careful scrutiny, find that just the opposite is true.

- The benefits of diversification may be realized only over the long term. It often takes time for you to fully appreciate the value of diversification.

INVESTMENT STRATEGIES

Some Terrible Truths

- Investment terminology and descriptions vary so greatly that investors may not be able to clearly understand the investment strategy they are using.

- Even those investors who are satisfied with their investment returns may be using an investment strategy that is unsuitable for them in the long term.

- Many investors are not psychologically suited to the investment strategy they have chosen.

- Mutual funds may change their investment styles without their investors being made aware of it.

What investment strategy are you using? Someone who invests money, whether he buys mutual funds, individual stocks, bonds, or CDs—whether he invests individually or through an investment advisor or money manager—simultaneously chooses an investment strategy. When selecting individual investments such as mutual funds for a portfolio, it is essential to first clearly understand what investment strategy is being used.

Simply defined, an investment strategy is a systematic method of making investment decisions. It may also be called an investment style. Countless investment choices are available today, including thousands of publicly traded stocks, mutual funds, private money managers, and bonds. In most cases, however, we can classify an investment into one of four categories of fundamental strategies. Examining these four strategies can give you insight, both to help you better understand your current investments, and also to select future investments.

The Importance of Knowing Investment Strategy

Most investors today own mutual funds, which are managed by professionals with various investment approaches. Clearly understanding the investment strategies that could be used by those funds can help you implement and maintain a well-conceived long-term investment portfolio.

It also will help you put into perspective the sometimes overwhelming assortment of financial advice given by commentators, columnists, investment newsletters, online services, books, magazines, and financial sales literature that can promote overly simplistic methods of achieving financial security.

Many investors may not have paid close attention to investment strategy because the returns from the U.S. stock markets have been remarkably favorable over the past two decades. From 1977 through 1996, the S&P 500 has provided investors with an average annual compound return of 14.6 percent—*40 percent higher* than its historical 10.7 percent average. At the same time, the standard deviation (which measures the up and down market volatility) for the S&P 500 has been *33 percent less* than its historical average. In addition,

Chart 8-1 illustrates that the volatility was *almost all on the positive side.*

This prolonged period of higher-than-average returns in combination with one-third less volatility could cause investors to have unrealistic expectations and ignore their choice of investment strategy. However, should the favorable investment climate change and bring a prolonged down market, millions of investors will become more clearly focused on their investment strategy. Unfortunately, it may be too late to correct the situation if they discover that the original strategy that was implemented was unsuitable.

Chart 8-1
Annual Returns of S&P 500 (1977-1996)

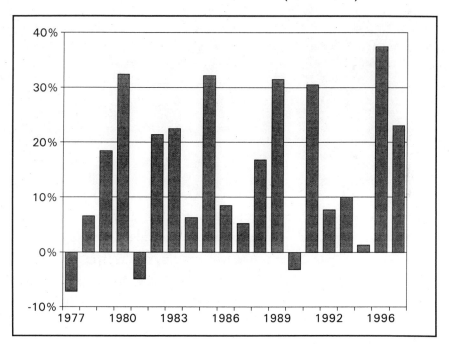

Pick Your Sport Carefully

Choosing an investment strategy without having a clear understanding of its characteristics is similar to taking up a sport without understanding its demands. People often try a sport and immediately have favorable experiences pursuing it. In some cases, however, they may not be physically or psychologically suited to it over the long term. For example, they may not have sound knees or elbows or, just as important, they may not have the temperament necessary to play the sport. Even if their initial experiences were positive, they may have chosen a sport that over a period of years could leave them with permanent injuries; or if their game were to go bad, they could become frustrated, resulting in irrational play. The same can be said of an investment strategy. It is possible to pick an investment strategy that from the very beginning was unsuitable for that investor. Yet, if that strategy provides positive returns at the outset, an investor may be led to persist, even though this may result in long-term failure.

In This Chapter...

We will examine the characteristics of the four fundamental investment styles that underlie all portfolios. We will see how they differ from each other, and then review examples of investments that fit within each strategy. Then we will examine prospectuses, mutual fund reports and other sources of information that can help us determine which strategy or strategies are being used. Using mutual funds as examples, we'll explore whether the stated strategy and the actual strategy are one and the same. Finally, we'll consider how an investor could select one investment style only to discover later that it had been modified without their knowledge.

Four Primary Investment Strategies

Investors may have heard mutual funds, stocks, bonds, and other investments characterized as "growth," "value," "income," "high yield," "balanced" and other terms. Money managers are often described as "aggressive," "conservative," or "contrarian." However, we must probe beyond these descriptions to identify the actual investment strategies we, our advisors or our mutual fund managers are really using. All the possible strategies are too numerous to list, but most of them fit within four primary categories: Security Selection, Market Timing, Security Selection with Market Timing, and No Security Selection or Market Timing.

Table 8-1

Security Selection **1**	Market Timing **2**
3 Security Selection with Market Timing	**4** No Security Selection or Market Timing

Many investors have more than one of these investment strategies in their portfolios; some even have all four. So let's examine each of them, and identify the types of investments that can fit into each category.

Box One: Security Selection

Security selection is probably the strategy most commonly used by individual investors, mutual fund managers, investment advisors, stock brokers, and professional money managers. Whether you buy a share of stock in AT&T, a CD from your local bank, a government bond, or gold, you have "selected" or chosen that individual investment over all others available. While security selection can be used to choose investments in any asset class, it is most commonly associated with the selection of stocks, so in our examples we will use stocks.

Professional investors who use security selection attempt to identify the stocks of companies or industries they believe will outperform others. Various techniques can be used to choose individual stocks, but the most commonly used methods are called *fundamental analysis* and *technical analysis*.

Fundamental Analysis

Fundamental analysis is used by most Wall Street security analysts. It is based on the idea that the best time to buy a stock is when the price is below what one's research indicates it is currently worth or should be worth in the future.

Fundamental analysis evaluates many aspects of a company. It looks at a company's book value, cash flow, current earnings, expected earnings growth rate, types and level of debt, the industry group the company is in, and the price-to-earnings ratio of its stock. Analysts want to know whether the company is in a growing industry, a mature industry, or a declining industry. They are interested in the strength and quality of the company's management, the stability of its workforce, customers' product loyalty, the company's emphasis on research and development, the level of competition in its industry, how the particular company's products compare with the competition, existing or potential lawsuits, and other factors that might affect the company's worth. Fundamental analysis generally focuses on two methods of selecting stocks: value and growth.

Value Analysis

Those who use value analysis are the investment world's equivalent of bargain hunters. They attempt to buy stocks that currently are selling below what the analysts perceive to be their value. An analyst may believe that a stock is undervalued for a variety of reasons including management changes, industry downturns, delays in getting a new product to market, a seasonal slump, a product recall, or simply belonging to an industry currently out of favor with investors.

Picture the following: you are an analyst focusing on value and have carefully evaluated a company. You conclude that its stock is worth $50 per share. When you check the newspaper, you discover that it is selling for $40 per share. You immediately buy it, because you believe this stock is undervalued and you expect the price to eventually increase to what you consider to be the real market value, $50 per share. By choosing a stock in this manner, you are using fundamental analysis with *value* as your criterion for selection.

Growth Analysis

Those who use growth analysis search for individual stocks or industry groups they think have excellent prospects for future growth in earnings and profits. They may say, "We feel this company is poised for rapid growth." An analyst focusing on growth studies profit margins, market trends, demographics, and company earnings, along with other factors, and then projects a potential future value for the company's stock. While the value analyst is concerned with what the stock is selling for today, the growth analyst is focused on what he or she believes the stock will sell for in the future.

Assume you now are an analyst focusing on growth. You have analyzed a company whose stock is selling today for $25 a share. After evaluating the company, you conclude that it has excellent potential for growth and earnings, and you believe its stock price will increase significantly in the future. Thus, you decide to buy that stock.

Now that we have covered two of the methods that fundamental analysis uses to select stocks—value and growth—let's move on to another method of security selection, technical analysis.

Technical Analysis

Technical analysis involves looking at many factors in selecting stocks for purchase, which are different from those used for fundamental analysis. Analysts who use a technical approach are sometimes called *chartists*. They are not interested in looking at a company's book value, cash flow, or expected earnings. Instead, they track a stock's daily price, the number of shares traded, and the percentage change in the stock's price and volume, then create complex charts and graphs reflecting this information.

They then analyze these charts, graphs and other indicators in an attempt to discover recurring and predictable patterns in stock prices that may enable them to forecast future price changes. If a particular pattern emerges, these analysts will buy or sell the stock. For example, an analyst who uses technical analysis may decide to buy a particular stock if its price drops below $12 per share, and sell it if it climbs above $30 per share.

Technical analysis involves many different methods of stock selection, but all of them share one distinctive feature: the use of stock price movements to determine whether to buy or sell a particular stock.

Box Two: Market Timing

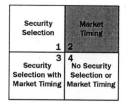

At the heart of a market-timing strategy is the belief that up and down movements in the securities markets can be forecasted accurately. A market timer attempts to shift investments before the market moves in the anticipated direction. The market timer strives to buy a particular asset before it goes up and to sell it before it goes down.

When interviewed in magazines or on television, market timers tell us they are "in the market" or "out of the market," based on where they believe "markets are headed." Many individual investors may not even be aware that they are pursuing a market-timing strategy with their investments. If you ask investors whether they use market timing, they respond "no"; yet it is not uncommon to hear these same people say, "I'm not investing in the market now because it's too high," or "I'm thinking about putting some money into the market now; this is a terrific time to buy."

Market timing is not limited to stocks; many investors use similar timing strategies with bonds. In that case, they attempt to forecast changes in interest rates. They know, as we discussed in the Volatility chapter, that bond values will decrease when interest rates exceed what the bond is yielding and values will increase when the interest rates are lower. Thus, bond timers buy bonds if they believe interest rates will decline, and they sell bonds if they believe interest rates are headed higher.

Investors have devised hundreds of methods to try to predict stock and bond markets. These range from very sophisticated, disciplined systems that diligently monitor various economic indicators to whimsical ones that forecast future stock prices by tracking sunspots, moon cycles and hemlines. A popular financial book, *A Random Walk Down Wall Street* by Burton Malkiel, offers the following comment:

> *"The attempt to predict accurately the future course of stock prices and thus the appropriate time to buy or sell a stock must rank as one of [our] most persistent endeavors. This search for the golden egg has spawned a variety of methods ranging from the scientific to the occult."*

Box Three: Security Selection with Market Timing

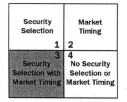

It is not unusual to find investors, advisors and mutual fund managers using both security selection and market timing simultaneously in their attempts to earn higher returns. For example, an investor may purchase an individual stock, believing it to be undervalued. The stock subsequently goes up in value. At that point the same investor feels the overall stock market is poised for a significant decline. Therefore, even though the investor doesn't think the stock itself is overvalued, he still sells it.

Another example of using both security selection and market timing would be a mutual fund that chooses to buy stocks as part of its portfolio. The fund generally limits the stocks in its portfolio to approximately 50 companies it anticipates are poised for substantial long-term growth. The fund currently allocates approximately 60 percent of its investments to stocks, 35 percent to bonds, and the remaining 5 percent to cash.

Suppose the fund manager believes the overall stock market has become significantly overvalued. As a result, he decreases the portfolio's allocation from 60 percent in stocks to 50 percent, while increasing his cash position from 5 percent to 15 percent. If the market should go down as he anticipates, he will at some future point move back to his original allocation of 60 percent in stocks and 5 percent in cash. This fund manager is using both security selection and market timing as a part of his overall investment strategy.

Box Four: No Security Selection or Market Timing

The fourth fundamental investment strategy does not use security selection, market timing or any combination of the two for selecting investments. What are examples of this strategy? If you invest your money in certificates of deposit and keep renewing them at maturity, irrespective of current interest rates or the availability of other investments, you probably are not relying on timing or security selection. Placing money in a money market account—which is, generally speaking, what most investors do with the cash component of their portfolios—also fits in this category.

Another category of investment that falls into the no security selection or market timing strategy is a type of a mutual fund called an index fund. A stock index fund buys all the stocks in a particular index and holds them regardless of whether they go up or down in value. For example, an index fund that tracks the S&P 500 Index buys all the stocks listed in that index. Since this strategy employs no market timing methods, the fund remains invested in those same stocks at all times. The fund buys a new stock only when a new company is added to the S&P 500, and it sells a stock only when a company is removed from the S&P 500. You may see an index fund described as "fully invested," which means the fund holds very little cash.

Some index funds invest in bonds. At least one index fund represents almost every major asset class, i.e., small-company stocks, international stocks, emerging markets, short-term bonds, intermediate-term bonds, and long-term bonds.

Investors who use index funds generally believe it is difficult to successfully select securities or time markets on a consistent long-term basis. Index fund investors also give up the hope of beating the market. A true index fund cannot beat the market because it is the market.

Indexing was first used by institutional investors in 1971 and by the mutual fund industry in 1976. More than 10 percent of the market value of all U.S. stocks is currently invested using an index strategy.

Only the Beginning

The preceding descriptions of the four basic investment strategies represent only a piece of a much larger puzzle. Each fundamental strategy has many substrategies, variations, focuses, and styles. For example, the security selection strategy contains fundamental and technical analysis, growth and value styles or choosing small-company stocks rather than large-company stocks. In market timing, some investors may base their market timing decisions on perceptions of relative value between asset classes ("bonds are a better value than stocks right now") or on their reading of economic indicators ("from our forecasts of the economy, we think the outlook for stocks is good for the future"). Entire books have been written on just one investment strategy or style of investing.

Which Box Or Boxes Do You Fall In?

Now that you have seen what the fundamental strategies are, you can look at your portfolios and see where your investments fit within the four-box matrix. If you own individual stocks or bonds, these fall in Box One, Security Selection. Money you have invested in CDs or other cash equivalents and kept there for extended periods goes in Box Four, No Security Selection or Market Timing. If you own a mutual fund that uses both stock picking and market timing, and another fund that only uses market timing, these fit into Boxes Three and Two, respectively. It is not unusual to have investments in a portfolio that fit into more than one, or even all four, investment strategies.

Unfortunately, it is not always easy to determine what strategies your advisors or mutual fund managers are actually following. With the enormous growth of the mutual fund industry and self-directed 401(k)s and other retirement plans, it's imperative that investors have a clear understanding of investment strategies before they select their investments.

Determining the Strategy of a Manager

How can investors verify what strategy their mutual fund or money manager is following? A number of sources can give investors the type of information they need. Each mutual fund is required by law to send you documents: a *prospectus* and a *statement of additional information*, which in most cases are complex booklets that include a description of how the fund intends to invest your money. In an attempt to determine or confirm a particular fund's strategy, we will look at some specific examples of prospectus language.

Unfortunately, the terminology and descriptions used by the industry to describe investment strategies don't always clearly or accurately reflect what the mutual fund manager is actually doing. This is not done to misinform or mislead, but is simply in keeping with financial industry definitions, standards, and practices. But as a result, investors sometimes think they have purchased a fund that uses one strategy when the fund is actually following a different one.

Reading the Fine Print

Prospectuses must comply with specific legal requirements, but the overwhelming majority do not give investors precise, discernible information in clear, unambiguous language. Thus, it is often difficult to clearly identify the strategy a particular fund or money manager is using. In addition, there is no guarantee that a strategy won't be modified in the future.

Perhaps the best sources of information available to the general public for determining a mutual fund's strategy are the reports provided by independent investment rating service companies such as Morningstar, Lipper and Value Line. Their reports are available through private subscription and in most public libraries. These companies compile extensive historical and current information on thousands of individual mutual funds. They issue reports that include classifying funds by category and style; historical return and risk measures (such as standard deviation); the name(s) of fund manager(s); the fund's inception date; and fund minimums for investment purchases. Rating service reports also give details on sector allocations (for example, what percentage is invested in certain industries, such as financial stocks), aggregate portfolio characteristics (price/ earnings ratios and capitalization for stocks, and maturity dates for bonds), top individual holdings of stocks or bonds, and geographic distribution of stocks around the world (e.g., the percentage invested in companies located in the U.S., Europe, and Asia).

The reports also incorporate statistical measurements of mutual funds' past performance and risk, and rate their performance relative to their peers and to indices. These reports give us a snapshot, at a given moment in time, of a fund's portfolio allocation, which can help determine how faithfully the fund is adhering to its stated investment philosophy. Later, we will use Morningstar reports as one source of information in determining a fund's investment strategy.

How can you determine what strategy your financial advisor, or private money manager is pursuing? One solution, of course, is to ask them. Another one is to retain a consulting firm that specializes in tracking and analyzing money managers. But the same concerns apply: *you must be sure you clearly understand the information being provided.* Thoroughly understanding the investment strategy recommended by an advisor is the first step in ensuring that the investment strategy is consistent with your long-term planning objectives, because the advisor's strategy becomes *your* strategy.

Confirming a Mutual Fund's Strategy

The following exercises are designed to help you sort through different types of information you may encounter so that you can determine the investment strategy of your current and future investments. To do this, we will look at various sources, including language from actual prospectuses and Morningstar reports on mutual funds that fit within each of our four categories of fundamental investment strategies. Although we will be using specific mutual funds as examples, they are *not* recommendations for readers of this book to purchase for their own portfolios.

Box One: Security Selection

Our first example involves an investor who plans to use security selection. The investor has chosen a mutual fund called Heartland Value. Let's see whether this investment meets the investor's goal of using security selection. Heartland's prospectus tells us:

> "Heartland Advisors selects *securities it considers to be underpriced* relative to a set of factors, including: price/earnings ratio; market price to book value; price/cash flow ratio; earnings growth; long term debt/capital; ...undervalued assets; ...technical analysis..." [italics added]

Investigating further, we look at Morningstar's report on Heartland. This indicates, in a number of places, that the fund pursues a security selection strategy, beginning with the fund description in the upper left-hand corner.

In the Portfolio Analysis section, Morningstar reports that Heartland holds 266 stocks, a further indication that the fund selects a limited number of individual securities that meet its investment criteria. The investment style matrix (shown in the lower right-hand portion of the report) tells us that the fund invests in small-company stocks and uses a value approach. Based on this review, we can

conclude that the Heartland Value fund fits into the Box One strategy
of Security Selection.

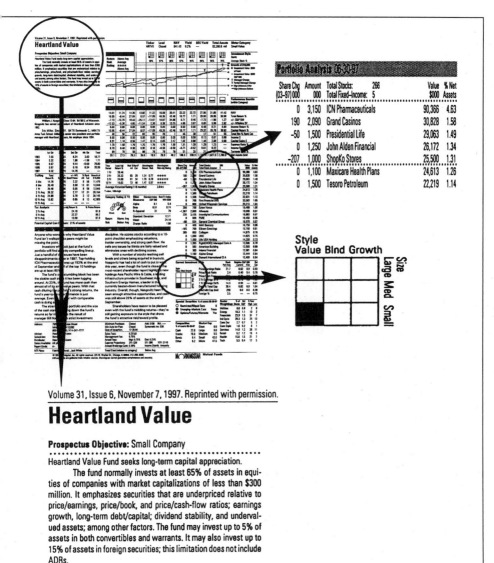

Volume 31, Issue 6, November 7, 1997. Reprinted with permission.

Heartland Value

Prospectus Objective: Small Company

Heartland Value Fund seeks long-term capital appreciation.
The fund normally invests at least 65% of assets in equities of companies with market capitalizations of less than $300
million. It emphasizes securities that are underpriced relative to
price/earnings, price/book, and price/cash-flow ratios; earnings
growth, long-term debt/capital; dividend stability, and undervalued assets; among other factors. The fund may invest up to 5% of
assets in both convertibles and warrants. It may also invest up to
15% of assets in foreign securities; this limitation does not include
ADRs.

Now let's look at another fund, American Century-20th Century Growth Investors, and see whether this investment also belongs in Box One. In looking at this mutual fund's prospectus, we find the following language:

"[The fund normally invests] in securities, primarily common stocks, that meet *certain fundamental and technical standards of selection* and have, in the opinion of ... management, *better-than-average potential for appreciation.*" [italics added]

The prospectus language indicates that the fund manager uses security selection. It does not give any indication that a market timing strategy may be involved. But even though we may be satisfied that the fund manager is using security selection, prudence dictates we investigate the matter further.

So our next step is to turn to the Morningstar report on this fund. In the upper left-hand corner under "Prospectus Objective" the Morningstar report states:

"The fund normally invests substantially all assets in equity securities of large, established companies that meet its standards of earnings and revenue growth."

From the Portfolio Analysis in the middle section of right-hand side of the page, we find that the fund owns 63 stocks. We already know that there are thousands of stocks available for purchase. The fact that this fund, with more than $5 billion in assets, owns just 63 stocks indicates a stringent level of security selection. Based on these pieces of information, we can conclude that the fund pursues a security selection strategy and indeed belongs in Box One.

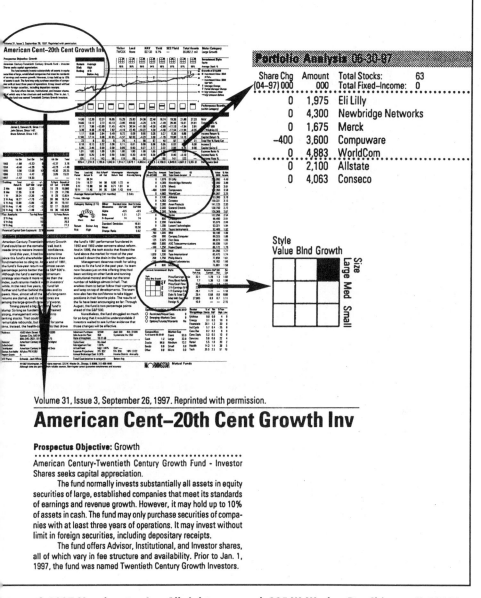

Volume 31, Issue 3, September 26, 1997. Reprinted with permission.

American Cent–20th Cent Growth Inv

Prospectus Objective: Growth

American Century-Twentieth Century Growth Fund - Investor Shares seeks capital appreciation.

The fund normally invests substantially all assets in equity securities of large, established companies that meet its standards of earnings and revenue growth. However, it may hold up to 10% of assets in cash. The fund may only purchase securities of companies with at least three years of operations. It may invest without limit in foreign securities, including depositary receipts.

The fund offers Advisor, Institutional, and Investor shares, all of which vary in fee structure and availability. Prior to Jan. 1, 1997, the fund was named Twentieth Century Growth Investors.

Box Two: Market Timing

How can you tell whether your mutual fund or money manager is using a market-timing strategy? Let's look at a bond fund, ISI Total Return U.S. Treasury. The prospectus tells us that the fund invests solely in U.S. Treasury bonds, bills, or notes. The prospectus also says the fund will change its portfolio composition based on its "expectations of future changes in interest rates."

Turning to the Morningstar report on this fund, we find in the Analysis section the following:

> "Manager Alan Medaugh runs this fund by *trying to predict the movement of interest rates* and adjusting duration... Medaugh bases his predictions on the ISI's economic surveys...Because the survey data can change frequently, *the fund's duration also changes often.*" [italics added]

Language from both the prospectus and the Morningstar report strongly indicates that the fund follows a market-timing strategy. Because the prospectus states that the portfolio's composition is based on the fund manager's "expectations" of future changes in interest rates, we know that the fund manager tries to predict interest rate movements. The Morningstar analysis, which says the fund manager attempts to predict interest rate moves and adjusts the fund's investments accordingly, corroborates that the fund manager is following the strategy stated in the prospectus.

Volume 31, Issue 1, August 29, 1997. Reprinted with permission.

ISI Total Return U.S. Treasury

Prospectus Objective: Government Treasury

ISI Total Return U.S. Treasury Fund Shares seeks total return consistent with relative stability of principal and current income. The fund invests solely in U.S. Treasury securities and in repurchase agreements fully collateralized by U.S. Treasury securities. It may invest in the entire range of maturities offered by such securities.

Prior to April 15, 1991, the fund was named the C. J. Lawrence Total Return U.S. Treasury Fund. The fund has an additional class of shares named Flag Investors Total Return U.S. Treasury Fund Shares; these shares are sold through Alex Brown with a 4.5% maximum load.

Analysis by Maciej Kowara 08-15-97

ISI Total Return U.S. Treasury Fund Shares goes through lots of motions, but doesn't move any faster than its average peer.

Manager Alan Medaugh runs this fund by trying to predict the movement of interest rates and adjusting duration, which usually stays between six and eight years. Medaugh bases his predictions on the ISI's economic surveys; these include company surveys, which allow him to gauge the strength of the economy, and bond-manager surveys, which he uses as a contrarian indicator. Because the survey data can change frequently, the fund's duration also changes often.

For all this activity, the fund's returns are only about average. There are two reasons for this. First, despite its flexibility, the fund's duration is usually shorter than its average peer's. While this offers more protection in bear markets, it also limits the fund's upside potential when rates are falling. (On the positive side, this duration stance also accounts for the fund's moderate risk scores.) More important, however, Medaugh's success at timing rates has been mixed. He shortened duration early in 1994, for example, which led to the fund's best relative performance in its history. Shortening duration in 1992's rally, by contrast, was a mistake that caused the fund's worst annual relative performance.

So far this year, Medaugh's timing has worked out. He started the year rather short and stayed so until April, when he gradually extended duration to 7.8 years. These moves coincided with changes in interest rates. Although his timing has been right on the money, the fund's shorter-than-average duration has once again acted as somewhat of a brake on returns. Thus, the fund is again in the middle of the category.

This mixed record, with hits compensating for misses, adds up to a decent, but by no means outstanding, long-term government fund.

Another indication of whether a fund is pursuing a market-timing strategy is the percentage of its assets held in cash. As we discussed earlier, when market timers are out of the market, they generally keep their funds in cash so they can quickly move back into the market when they believe the "time is right." The following chart from data supplied by the fund, shows how ISI's percentage of assets invested in cash fluctuated between 1992 through 1997.

Table 8-2
ISI Total Return U.S. Treasury Fund

Date	Percent in Cash
January 1992	3.0%
April 1992	22.6%
September 1992	18.9%
December 1992	7.3%
April 1993	3.0%
October 1993	3.6%
December 1993	15.8%
March 1994	21.7%
June 1994	4.6%
September 1994	21.5%
March 1995	1.4%
June 1995	0.9%
September 1995	8.3%
December 1995	3.3%
April 1996	17.0%
August 1997	25.0%

When we combine the information from the cash fluctuation chart with the clues from the prospectus and the Morningstar report, we can reasonably conclude that the ISI Total Return U.S. Treasury mutual fund relies to some extent on market-timing strategies.

Box Three: Security Selection with Market Timing

The Zweig Series Strategy A fund provides an example of a fund that uses a combination of security selection and market timing. Its prospectus states that the fund can move the portfolio completely to cash in an attempt to avoid market risk. In a phone conversation, the fund manager disclosed the historical information on the fund illustrated in Table 8-3.

Table 8-3
Zweig Series Strategy A Fund

Date	Percentage in Stocks	Percentage in Cash
November 11, 1993	62%	38%
March 3, 1994	41%	59%
December 31, 1995	76%	24%
July 30, 1996	92%	8%
July 17, 1997	85%	15%

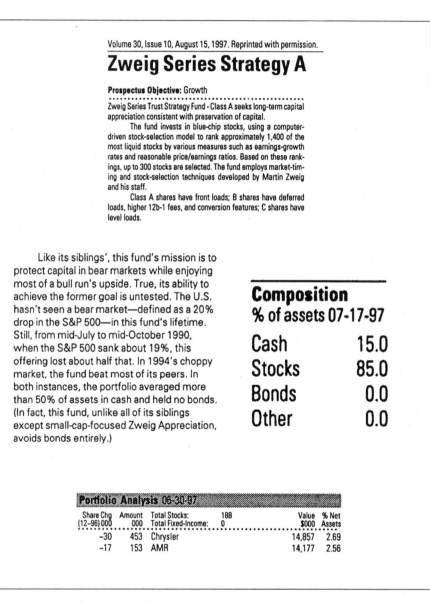

Volume 30, Issue 10, August 15, 1997. Reprinted with permission.

Zweig Series Strategy A

Prospectus Objective: Growth

Zweig Series Trust Strategy Fund - Class A seeks long-term capital appreciation consistent with preservation of capital.

The fund invests in blue-chip stocks, using a computer-driven stock-selection model to rank approximately 1,400 of the most liquid stocks by various measures such as earnings-growth rates and reasonable price/earnings ratios. Based on these rankings, up to 300 stocks are selected. The fund employs market-timing and stock-selection techniques developed by Martin Zweig and his staff.

Class A shares have front loads; B shares have deferred loads, higher 12b-1 fees, and conversion features; C shares have level loads.

Like its siblings', this fund's mission is to protect capital in bear markets while enjoying most of a bull run's upside. True, its ability to achieve the former goal is untested. The U.S. hasn't seen a bear market—defined as a 20% drop in the S&P 500—in this fund's lifetime. Still, from mid-July to mid-October 1990, when the S&P 500 sank about 19%, this offering lost about half that. In 1994's choppy market, the fund beat most of its peers. In both instances, the portfolio averaged more than 50% of assets in cash and held no bonds. (In fact, this fund, unlike all of its siblings except small-cap-focused Zweig Appreciation, avoids bonds entirely.)

Composition
% of assets 07-17-97

Cash	15.0
Stocks	85.0
Bonds	0.0
Other	0.0

Portfolio Analysis 06-30-97

Share Chg (12–96) 000	Amount 000	Total Stocks: Total Fixed-Income:	188 0	Value $000	% Net Assets
–30	453	Chrysler		14,857	2.69
–17	153	AMR		14,177	2.56

This fluctuation in the percentage of assets held in cash strongly suggests that the fund manager is using market-timing techniques. In addition, the Morningstar report's description of the fund states: "The fund employs market-timing and stock-selection techniques..." The Analysis section notes that in 1990 and 1994, the fund averaged more than 50 percent cash. In the upper left-hand corner we find: "The fund invests in blue-chip stocks, using a computer-driven stock-selection model to rank approximately 1,400 of the most liquid stocks by various methods... " The report shows that the fund owns only 188 stocks, so security selection clearly is being employed. Putting the information together, we find that this fund is managed with a combination of security selection and market-timing strategies.

Box Four: No Security Selection or Market Timing

As we saw earlier, various types of investments may fall into Box Four, ranging from CDs or money market accounts to stock and bond index mutual funds. Let's look at an example of a mutual fund that invests in large-company stocks but uses neither security selection or market timing. The Vanguard Index Trust 500 Portfolio is such a fund. The fund's prospectus contains the following statement:

> "The 500 Portfolio seeks to replicate the aggregate price and yield performance of the Standard & Poors 500 Composite Stock Price Index, an index which emphasizes large-capitalization companies... [The] Portfolio attempts to remain fully invested in common stocks."

This fund replicates the performance of the S&P 500 Index by buying all the stocks that make up the index. The Morningstar report for the Vanguard Index 500 shows that the fund is 98.2 percent invested in stocks. The prospectus language and the minimal cash position confirm our notion that the fund is not engaged in market-timing activities. Because the stocks purchased replicate a predetermined index, this fund clearly falls into Box Four as it does not use security selection or market timing as its investment strategy.

Index funds are also available for other asset classes. Some funds, for example, buy only large-company stocks across the Pacific Rim nations, or large-company European stocks. Others buy bonds, real estate, small-company U.S. stocks, or international stocks based on an index.

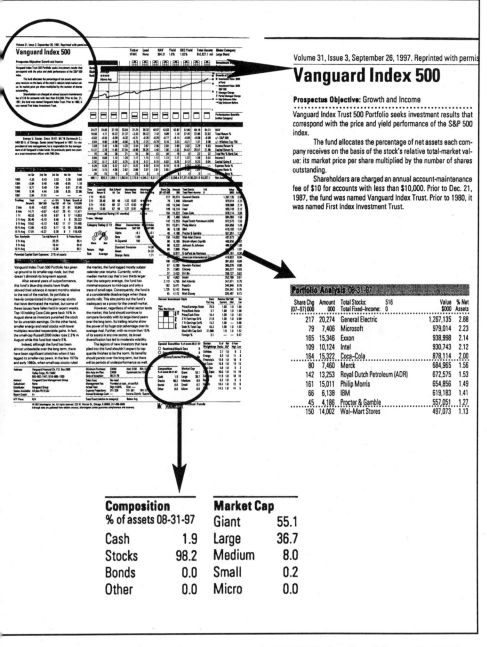

Volume 31, Issue 3, September 26, 1997. Reprinted with permis

Vanguard Index 500

Prospectus Objective: Growth and Income

Vanguard Index Trust 500 Portfolio seeks investment results that correspond with the price and yield performance of the S&P 500 index.

The fund allocates the percentage of net assets each company receives on the basis of the stock's relative total-market value: its market price per share multiplied by the number of shares outstanding.

Shareholders are charged an annual account-maintenance fee of $10 for accounts with less than $10,000. Prior to Dec. 21, 1987, the fund was named Vanguard Index Trust. Prior to 1980, it was named First Index Investment Trust.

Portfolio Analysis 08-31-97

Share Chg (07-97)	Amount 000	Total Stocks: 516 Total Fixed-Income: 0	Value $000	% Net Assets
217	20,274	General Electric	1,267,135	2.88
79	7,406	Microsoft	979,014	2.23
165	15,346	Exxon	938,998	2.14
109	10,124	Intel	930,743	2.12
164	15,322	Coca-Cola	878,114	2.00
80	7,460	Merck	684,965	1.56
142	13,253	Royal Dutch Petroleum (ADR)	672,575	1.53
161	15,011	Philip Morris	654,856	1.49
66	6,139	IBM	619,183	1.41
45	4,186	Procter & Gamble	557,051	1.27
150	14,002	Wal-Mart Stores	497,073	1.13

Composition
% of assets 08-31-97

Cash	1.9
Stocks	98.2
Bonds	0.0
Other	0.0

Market Cap

Giant	55.1
Large	36.7
Medium	8.0
Small	0.2
Micro	0.0

How can we tell whether a fund fits into Box Four? In many cases, the word "index" appears in the name of the fund. In addition, most index funds have two things in common. First, they seek to replicate the risk and return characteristics of a given index, without regard to such fundamental or technical selection criteria as price/earnings ratio, cash flow, book value, industry outlook, or management changes. Second, they stay fully invested, rather than trying to anticipate rising or falling markets.

It is important to note that an investor could choose to buy an index fund and still not fit into Box Four. Such an investor might be a market timer or tactical asset allocator whose investment strategy was not only to invest in large-company stocks but also to attempt to anticipate when markets will go up or decline in value. This type of strategy might involve using an index fund as a vehicle for buying a segment of the market when the investor feels that segment will increase in value and selling it when he expects it to decline. This clearly would be a market-timing investment strategy that belongs in Box Two.

Understanding Your Strategy In Advance

Many individuals second guess their investment strategy. For example, an investor who wants to put part of his portfolio into large-company U.S. stocks may invest money in an S&P 500 index fund, because he believes he will be satisfied to get the average market return. Later, however, he might be upset that many other mutual funds have outperformed his index fund. A second investor, also wanting to invest a portion of his portfolio in large-company U.S. stocks, may choose a fund that uses security selection in an attempt to beat the average return of the market. Subsequently, however, this fund might under perform the market average. In either case, investors may feel dissatisfied with their investment performance and start to second-guess their choices. But if those investors had clearly understood in advance the characteristics of the investment strategy chosen, they wouldn't have been surprised by either outcome.

Second-Guessing Could Be Costly

When investors become unhappy with the performance of their investments, they often want to change to a new strategy that is currently providing higher returns. But investors who constantly change from one strategy to another may be setting themselves up for an investment and psychological roller-coaster ride. This ride could be avoided if they clearly understand the characteristics and potential outcomes of their investment strategy before it is adopted. Continual changes in investment strategies usually result in inferior returns for most investors.

Shifting Sands:
Your Mutual Fund May Change Its Style

Investors should remember that even after they have selected an investment using a specific investment style, it is not unusual for that style to change. As a result, after some time has passed, an investment could have little resemblance to what was first chosen. Let's consider some mutual funds to illustrate this point.

An investor who bought 20th Century Ultra Fund (later renamed American Century-20th Century Ultra Investment Fund) in 1989 with the objective of owning small-company stocks would have seen the fund's composition change so radically that by 1995, it was classified as a large-company stock fund.

The opposite would occur to someone who invested in 1991 in the Strong Common Stock fund—a large-company stock fund. By the next year, investors found themselves owning a small-company stock fund. Since 1994, the fund has been classified as a mid-cap stock fund.

There are other ways an investment style could shift. Funds may change their selection process from growth to value or from value to growth. Take Fidelity Capital Appreciation, which has exhibited significant style swings over the past seven years. From 1989 to 1992, its management followed a value strategy to select investments. In 1993 it used a blend of value and growth; in 1994 it shifted to pure growth; in 1995 it changed back to pure value; and in 1996 it was again modified to its current blend of value and growth.

There could be numerous reasons for major style or strategy changes, such as a change in the fund's manager. In some cases a new manager may decide to emphasize market timing significantly more than his or her predecessor, or the manager may greatly increase or reduce the number of stocks held in the fund's portfolio. Or perhaps a tremendous influx of money into the fund from new investors occurs, making it difficult for the manager to purchase investments that fit the fund's original selection criteria, so the manager responds by adding different types of investments. Or because a fund has recently under-performed competing funds, the manager may choose a different investment style in hopes of achieving higher returns.

The kind of changes we have noted are not necessarily unanticipated or unwelcomed by investors. Originally, an investor may have selected the fund manager specifically because that manager promised to shift the investment style or strategy to meet performance goals.

Regardless, it is important to be aware that these changes can occur, because they could alter an investor's overall portfolio design or change a portfolio's level of diversification. When change occurs, the investor (or their advisor) needs to decide whether it is in the investor's best interests to maintain these investments as a part of the portfolio.

Summary: Tools for the Savvy Investor

- By knowing the characteristics of the four fundamental investment strategies, you can review your portfolio to see into which categories your investments fall.

- An awareness of different investment strategies can also help you or your advisor when selecting future investments.

- Understanding investment strategies can help you understand the decision processes used by mutual fund managers and other investment advisors.

- A clear understanding of your own investment strategy or strategies can better prepare you to weather the emotional challenges that come with investing, and can help you avoid second-guessing.

- Given the growth of 401(k) plans and the range of investment selections offered, identifying which of the four categories of investment strategies an investment falls into can help you in your selection process, if you are a participant in a 401(k) plan.

- Before you choose an investment for your portfolio, independent sources of information can be used to verify the investment strategy to see if it is appropriate for you.

SELECTED INVESTMENT ISSUES

Some Terrible Truths

- Investment and retirement planning software sometimes creates more problems than it solves.

- Inefficient investment of tax-deferred and taxable assets generates needless taxes.

- The over simplification of lifecyle or age-based investing causes many investors to disregard other important investment principles.

- Most investors have never tried to dollar cost average through a prolonged down stock market.

- Often, not enough time is spent on asset allocation decisions such as rebalancing after a portfolio's initial design.

Literally hundreds of investment issues could have been included in this chapter. However, I believe the following five will sooner or later impact nearly all investors and advisors:

- computer programs for investment and retirement planning,

- dollar cost averaging,

- portfolio allocations and rebalancing,

- tax-efficient investing, and

- lifecyle investing.

Each of these topics can have far-ranging implications for investors. In lifecyle investing, for instance, critical issues regarding diversification and risk surface. In discussing computer software, the problem of how emotions can control investment policy is addressed. Thus, the topics have been chosen for this chapter in order to help investors identify other important investment issues which must be considered before investment decisions are made.

COMPUTER PROGRAMS FOR INVESTMENT AND RETIREMENT DECISIONS

With the explosion in the number of people using computers, we have seen a significant increase in the availability and use of retirement- and investment-planning software programs offered by software companies, investment firms, and Internet sites. In addition, some corporations provide these programs for their employees. The use of software programs as planning tools will continue to increase, and the programs will become more sophisticated.

Many people use these programs to make critical decisions such as when and whether they can afford to retire and what percentages of their portfolios they should allocate among stocks, bonds, and other asset classes. They also use the programs to assess whether they should be investing more conservatively or aggressively to meet specific goals.

While financial software can be an excellent tool for some individuals, using this technology to make retirement and investment decisions also raises unexpected planning issues. In the worst case, poorly designed or improperly used programs can lure investors into making harmful decisions. To get the best use from an investment planning program, *you must first carefully examine the assumptions built into the programs* and then determine whether or not they are realistic. Just as important, you must be careful when you provide the personal information the program asks you to furnish.

These programs can contain many flaws and limitations. Understanding some of their potential limitations can be key for those who use them in their planning. Whether or not these specific problems are present in the software you are currently using, this examination can alert you to the type of general planning issues you might otherwise overlook.

For the Computerless Too

Even if you are not currently using a computer program to assist you in your retirement and investment planning, the following discussion of computer-related issues can be extremely helpful in focusing your attention on important retirement and investment decisions.

Life Expectancy

Retirement planning software must make an assumption about how long you will live. One of the most popular programs asks users about their personal health. It lets them choose among "excellent," "good," "fair," and "poor," then gives an estimated life expectancy. For example, if a 40-year-old male answers "excellent," he is given a life expectancy of 82 years. If he answers "poor," the program assumes he will live until age 80—a difference in life expectancy of only two years. Think about that. A young individual who believes his health is poor may be concerned about a chronic medical problem such as diabetes or a heart condition. Is it realistic for this program to assume that an individual who attests to being in poor health will have nearly the same life expectancy as an individual who considers himself to be in excellent health?

Incredibly, some programs make no distinction between the life expectancy of a single person and that of a couple, which contradicts basic data on life expectancies. As we saw in the Time Horizons chapter, the surviving member of a couple is projected to have a significantly longer life expectancy than a single individual.

In addition, most programs don't encourage users to consider their own family genetic information, and yet that information may provide important clues to their life expectancy. For example, an individual whose parents lived into their 90s is given a significant chance of also living that long. But in fact, the majority of computer programs do not include personal or family genetic profiles; consequently, the projections they generate may be based on assumptions that are unrealistic for your own unique planning.

The sensitivity of financial-planning software to varying assumptions about how long you will live has a significant impact on your overall retirement planning. In the few examples we have looked at, individuals easily could use unrealistic assumptions. As we saw in the chapters on Real Rates of Return and Time Horizons, the difference in the amount of assets needed to pay for retirement for an individual living just a few years longer than expected can be staggering.

Social Security

Software programs use a wide range of methods to calculate Social Security retirement benefits. In some, Social Security benefits are automatically included; others allow you to provide your own assumptions to override the computer's calculation of expected benefits. If your program does not allow you to override its automatic calculation, the estimates could be too high or too low. Case in point: one program bases its projection entirely on your current year's income. But Social Security benefits are calculated by including the majority of a person's working years; therefore, an estimate based on a single year's income can be significantly off.

Some investors do not want to include Social Security in their retirement projections at all, because they suspect benefits no longer will be available when they retire. Others expect to receive their full benefits, and still others may want to modify the projected amount in some way. Whatever the assumed benefit, users must also consider how the software deals with the issue of future cost-of-living adjustments in Social Security benefits. The loss or reduction in the cost-of-living adjustment (COLA) at any point can result in a significant increase in the dollars necessary to fund retirement goals—often a difference of hundreds of thousands of dollars.

Expected Investment Returns

Some software programs allow you to choose the rate of return you expect from your investments—say, from 1 percent to 20 percent—while others put constraints on unrealistic returns. Still other programs automatically calculate your expected returns based on the investment mix chosen.

Whether you choose the expected rate of return, or the program does it for you, overreliance on the built-in assumptions can be dangerous. For example, an individual may assume a 3 percent inflation rate and a 12 percent rate of investment return—*a 9 percent real rate of return* (the difference between the return and inflation). If that person wants to use assumptions that are consistent with historical real rates of return, and further wishes to invest in conservative fixed-income investments, then assuming a 9 percent rate of return over inflation would be unrealistic for long-term planning.

Another individual may be looking only at his personal investment experiences over a short period of time in developing assumptions to use for expected returns. But a person's recent investment returns may have been significantly higher than long-term historical averages. For example, the average annual compound return of the S&P 500 from 1980 to 1990 was 17.5 percent and from 1995 through 1997 was over 29 percent! Yet over the 72 years from 1926 through 1997, the S&P average was only 11.0 percent.

Other investors may have recently invested their money with a highly regarded mutual fund or money manager that has a short-term track record of 15 to 20 percent returns. These investors may be vulnerable to making overly optimistic assumptions about their future rates of returns, since human nature can lead them to believe similar returns will continue indefinitely in the future.

Software that is preprogrammed to give expected returns for stocks, bonds and other investment choices may base them on any of a number of historical time periods. It is important that investors know which historical periods are used. A program using historical data from 1975 through 1997 will have quite different results from one using data from 1926 through 1997.

Once they have identified the particular time period being used, investors can decide whether the expected returns are consistent with their own projections. Investors who rely on optimistic assumptions are often more prone to overreact to negative markets, which in turn could jeopardize their goal of accumulating enough assets to achieve their financial objectives.

Don't Overlook Your Frame of Mind

When making assumptions for retirement planning and financial software, investors must also be aware that recent experiences could dramatically impact their frame of mind on the day they sit down to use the software. For example, they may have received a job promotion or salary increase, or seen their investments perform beyond expectations. To these individuals, life is terrific and there is a feeling of invincibility.

On the other hand, some software users will have had career or investment setbacks, or experienced turmoil in their personal lives. Thus when using software, it is important to calmly sit back and make a conscious effort to keep either positive or negative short-term experiences from unduly influencing the assumptions you make regarding long-term projections.

Risk Tolerance

Let's say you perform a projection on your computer for retirement at age 60. The computer calculates that to achieve this goal, you should allocate your investments as follows: 80 percent in stock, 15 percent in debt/bonds, and 5 percent in cash/money market funds. But the computer has failed to ask whether you can tolerate the volatility of this portfolio over the long term—which you may or may not be able to do. Even if the program includes a risk tolerance questionnaire, it may not ask some extremely sensitive questions about your personal life that could make an enormous difference in building long-term portfolios.

How Reliable Are the Numbers?

When calculating long-term retirement projections, software programs can significantly differ in the way they calculate returns. Many investors choose to have a higher percentage of stocks in their portfolios in the years prior to retirement than in the years after retirement. Suppose an investor expects a 9 percent pre-retirement return and a 6 percent post-retirement return. How does the software handle this? Some programs average the returns over the entire investment period. Others separately calculate pre- and post-retirement time periods. In many programs it is difficult to tell how the returns are calculated. Different methods of calculation produce significantly diverse outcomes, so it is important to identify the method your software program uses.

Taxes

Tax rates before and after retirement can be a critical part of retirement planning and may affect your projections in a number of ways, so you need to know whether taxes are properly factored into the program.

One well-known program asks you to provide your pre- and post-retirement income tax rates. Other programs automatically reduce your post-retirement tax rate when you give your pre-retirement tax rate. Is this a realistic assumption? A large portion of retirement income for many people will come from withdrawals from retirement plans such as 401(k)s or IRAs. Since that income has not yet been taxed, and could be a significant amount each year, all retirees may not find themselves in a lower tax bracket after they retire. Does the software program give you the flexibility to deal with your individual tax situation?

Most individuals have some assets invested in tax-deferred retirement plans and have other assets in personal taxable accounts. Does your software allow you to distinguish between the tax treatment of the two types of accounts? Or does the program lump all of your assets together and force you to use one tax rate for the projection?

Changing Assumptions to Fit Our Expectations

When using software programs for retirement and investment decision-making, we must select a variety of assumptions, whether it be the investment rate of return, future spending level, rate of inflation or how long we expect to live. It is human nature to want to solve the problem or issue at hand. If the assumptions we initially use do not give us the outcome we wanted, we may be tempted to change the assumptions until we achieve that result.

To illustrate: suppose an individual wants to retire at age 62. He enters his assumptions into the computer, including his current assets, expected rate of return on investments, an expected inflation rate, his life expectancy and a savings rate. The program calculates that he will have to work until age 67, or he will outlive his assets. Because this is not the answer he wanted, he decides to lower the inflation rate by 1/2 percent and raise the portfolio return by 1 percent. With these slight modifications, the program projects he will be able to retire at age 65. So he continues to tinker with the numbers until the program calculates he can indeed retire at the desired age of 62. Making a few slight modifications in the assumptions may help us get the solution we want, but these seemingly minor changes may actually create an even bigger problem—projections that are not realistic.

Preparing Yourself for Different Outcomes

When using software to determine how much money it will take to reach a specific financial goal, we will come up with a specific number. But in reality, chances are the actual amount we will need will often be higher or lower. Various methods are available for software to use to estimate how much money is needed to reach financial goals.

Let's use college funding as an example. Suppose you want to know how much money you'll need to save for your child's four years of college education, which is expected to start in 10 years and cost $10,000 a year. To determine how much money you will need to save each year, you generally must estimate two numbers: an investment rate of return on the savings, and an inflation rate on the college cost. If you use a return of 8 percent and inflation of 6 percent, you will need to save about $5,300 each year over the next 15 years.

NOTE: *This number enables you to have the entire four years of college funded by the first year. The figure is slightly different if you plan to fund each year as it occurs.*

To illustrate the method we just used, let's assume we have two decks of cards: one deck represents investment returns, and the other deck represents inflation rates. The deck of cards representing investment returns has 8 percent marked on all 52 cards, while all 52 cards in the inflation deck have 6 percent on them. Each deck is shuffled and we draw one card from each deck 52 times until we have drawn all the cards. In this case each pair of cards we draw always consists of a combination of an 8 percent rate of return and a 6 percent rate of inflation for our college projection.

But no matter how carefully we select the rate of investment return and the inflation rate, we simply don't know what the actual rates will be in the future. So we might consider an alternative method, which encompasses a variety of rates of return and inflation. It attempts to determine the probable outcomes of different combinations of these rates in order to yield a number of answers to the savings goal question.

While this alternative approach also uses two decks of cards, one for investment returns and one for inflation rates, the decks are different. Instead of all 52 of the return cards having 8 percent return, and all 52 of the inflation cards having 6 percent inflation, there are different rates of return on the investment deck and different inflation rates on the other deck. Let's say that 40 of the cards in the investment deck have an 8 percent return, while the rest have differing returns—for example, cards with 6 percent, 9 percent, 3 percent and so on. The same thing would occur in the inflation deck. Thirty of the cards might have a 6 percent inflation rate, and the remaining cards have rates that are higher or lower. Once again, we shuffle each deck of cards and draw all 52 combinations from the two decks. If you visualize drawing all the cards from these decks, you won't get an 8 percent return with a 6 percent inflation rate all 52 times as we did with the first two decks.

According to the first method, you would need to save $5,300 per year to meet the college funding goal. When using the second method, and remembering that most cards in the investment deck are 8 percent and most cards in the inflation deck are 6 percent, we will still often pull cards that produce the same savings goal of $5,300. At times, however, we will draw different combinations of return and inflation, and calculations may produce annual savings goals ranging from $3,200 to $6,400. This second method provides worst-case and best-case scenarios for achieving our college funding goal. This method, which projects a range of outcomes depending on the assumptions, is referred to as a "Monte Carlo" simulation.

Regardless of whether you use a method that produces a range of outcomes or a single outcome for a particular objective, it is essential to remember that no matter how accurate you try to be in your assumptions, the likelihood of being *exactly* on target is small. Thus, it may be useful to run separate projections based on optimistic and pessimistic assumptions to better prepare yourself psychologically for the unexpected. We live in an unpredictable and uncertain world, and the use of the computer cannot change that. While the computer can be an excellent tool to assist in financial decision making, you must always be aware of its limitations.

DOLLAR COST AVERAGING

One well-known strategy for investing is called "dollar cost averaging," which is simply a method of investing on a regular basis. For example, you might invest $100 every month in a stock mutual fund over a period of time. By committing yourself to investing the same amount on a regular schedule, you ensure that you will buy more shares of the fund when its price is lower, and fewer when the price is higher. Many investors do this when they make monthly contributions to their 401(k) plans or other investment programs.

Because dollar cost averaging is based on systematically investing money over a period of time, it assumes you will continue to invest even when investments go down in value. When asked whether they have the discipline to stick with this strategy, most people respond, "Absolutely." However, most investors who use dollar cost averaging have not been tested by a prolonged down market, the last of which occurred in 1973-74.

Staying Committed Through Down Markets

Investors using dollar cost averaging need to go through the mental exercise of imagining themselves in the future systematically investing during declining markets that last a long time. While many investors believe they can meet this challenge, most have never had to face it. After all, the 1987 stock market "crash" lasted only 90 days. To help them maintain the discipline to successfully dollar cost average during a prolonged down market, investors must adopt this attitude: "Great, here's an opportunity to buy more shares with the same amount of money." However, investors will find this is much easier said than done.

Investors who choose to use dollar cost averaging must also consider (as we have discussed throughout this book) the personal volatility that may occur in their daily lives. When that personal volatility coincides with a down investment market, the discipline required of investors is much more difficult than what they perceive.

Lump Sum Investment Versus Dollar Cost Averaging

More and more people will be faced with the issue of how to invest a lump sum of money. It may come from an inheritance, a gift, a bonus at work, life insurance proceeds, sale of a business, a payout from a retirement plan or a legal settlement. Should you use some form of dollar cost averaging to invest this money or should you invest it all at once?

Investment experts have different opinions on this. Some believe that, based on statistical history, you would do better to invest all your money at once. But other respected advisors recommend investing in portions of the lump sum over some extended period of time, over months or a number of years.

Taking Your Lumps Is Never Easy

Before deciding whether to invest a lump sum at once or phase it in over a period of time, you must take into account the rest of your portfolio in order to make decisions consistent with your allocation among asset classes. At the same time, you can review and reevaluate your cash flow needs, future spending patterns, and other planning considerations. Failure to do this would be putting the cart before the horse.

One factor that prompts advisors to recommend dollar cost averaging is investors' emotions. Suppose you invest your lump sum in the stock market and then the market plummets in value. Psychologically, will you be able to tolerate seeing that money decline in value, particularly if it represents a significant portion of your total assets? And what if this substantial market loss coincides with your having suffered personal difficulties?

REBALANCING A PORTFOLIO

Once investors have allocated certain percentages of their portfolios to stocks, bonds, cash equivalents or other investments, they then need to decide whether or not to maintain their portfolio's original design over time. The research on portfolio performance (which we examined in the Investment Fundamentals and Historical Returns chapter) indicated that the asset allocation of a portfolio was the most important determinant of the variations of investment returns. But the rates of return of asset classes differ and will cause your portfolio's allocation to shift from its initial design. Choosing to maintain your original portfolio allocation or design is referred to as "rebalancing."

Let's use a simple example to illustrate rebalancing. Assume that your portfolio is designed to include 50 percent stocks and 50 percent fixed-income investments. The stocks could be invested in different asset classes, such as small-company stocks, large-company stocks, and international stocks. The fixed-income investments could be divided among bonds, Treasury bills, and money market accounts. Of course investors may choose to use mutual funds to purchase these investments.

In our hypothetical 50/50 portfolio, let's assume that over time market changes have caused the stock portion of the portfolio to significantly increase in value. As a result, the value of the stocks is now 60 percent of the portfolio and only 40 percent is in fixed-income investments. Since the original portfolio design was 50 percent each in stocks and fixed-income investments, you now have a decision to make: whether to leave the portfolio alone or rebalance it to the original percentage allocations. If you rebalance, you would sell a portion of your stocks and buy additional fixed-income investments. Chart 9-1 illustrates this.

Chart 9-1
Rebalancing a Portfolio
(Part 1)

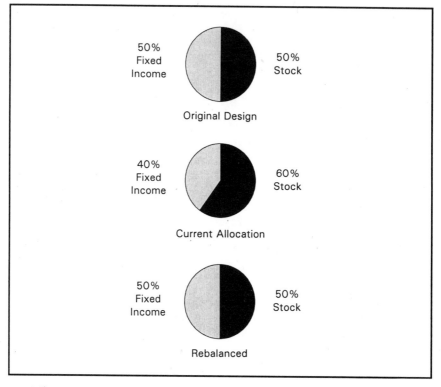

The same issue would have to be addressed regardless of the asset allocation, which could be 70 percent stocks and 30 percent fixed-income investments, 30 percent stocks and 70 percent fixed-income investments, or any other design.

On the other hand, market changes could cause the stock portion of your portfolio to decrease in value. So when you look at your portfolio sometime later, it might have changed to 40 percent stocks and 60 percent fixed-income investments. Again, should you wish to rebalance to your portfolio's original allocation of 50/50, you would need to sell a portion of your fixed-income investments and buy more stocks, as illustrated in Chart 9-2.

Chart 9-2
Rebalancing a Portfolio
(Part 2)

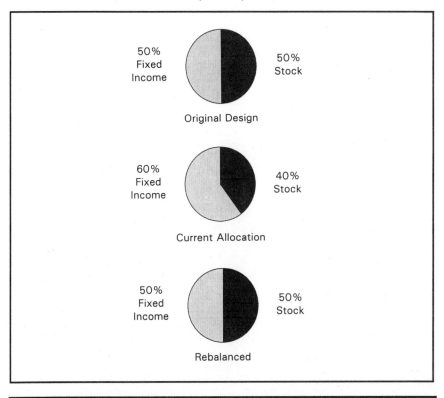

50% Fixed Income — 50% Stock — Original Design

60% Fixed Income — 40% Stock — Current Allocation

50% Fixed Income — 50% Stock — Rebalanced

Swimming Against the Tide

Rebalancing a portfolio requires you to exercise real discipline. For example, if the market is booming you must sell off a portion of what has gone up, and when the market drops you are required to buy what is going down. Thus, this strategy demands that you sell "winners" and buy what you may perceive as "losers!" This is contrary to human nature because our inclination is "to let the winners ride."

For investors or advisors who use portfolio rebalancing, it is important that they establish in advance some criteria for how often and on what basis they will rebalance. Take our hypothetical 50/50 portfolio. At what point should you rebalance—at 55/45, or 60/40, or some other ratio? Should you evaluate the portfolio's allocation monthly, quarterly, or annually? Other important considerations that affect the decision "whether and when to rebalance" include income tax consequences, transaction costs, and possible cash-flow needs.

Investors who choose to rebalance must remember that they are forfeiting the possibility of earning a higher overall long-term return. Let's compare two scenarios involving our hypothetical 50/50 port-folio. One scenario involves an investor who chooses to rebalance and the other an investor who leaves his portfolio alone. If stocks generate superior returns over a long period of time, the investor who rebalances will systematically sell off a portion of these higher-returning investments. The investor who simply leaves his portfolio alone will likely wind up (in this case) with a larger portfolio, due to the greater percentage of stocks. (Of course, he will also have the higher risk portfolio, and there is no guarantee the stocks will go up.)

Whether or not an investor chooses to rebalance a portfolio, there is another issue that must always be addressed. Regardless of what investment strategy is used, it is essential for investors to have an advance plan of what they might do under changing market conditions, whether up or down. This also serves as a reminder that even the most simple-appearing investment issues—when more closely examined—can be loaded with both technical and behavioral complexities.

ARE YOU INVESTING YOUR ASSETS TO BE TAX EFFICIENT?

Many individuals are responsible for investing both their personal (taxable) assets and their tax-deferred assets (such as those held in 401(k) plans or IRAs). Should taxable and tax-deferred assets be invested differently? Experts give different answers. Let's examine just one aspect of the dilemma—income tax efficiency. Considering the implications of the following example may encourage you to spend more time analyzing the tax implications of investing.

Suppose an individual is investing for retirement. This hypothetical investor has divided $200,000 between two mutual funds: $100,000 invested in Fund A inside a tax-deferred IRA account, and $100,000 of taxable personal assets invested in Fund B. Both mutual funds invest in large-company stocks.

The manager of Fund A, inside the tax-deferred IRA account, pursues an investment objective that involves buying stocks and holding them for long periods of time—a "buy and hold" strategy. The manager of Fund B buys stocks in companies that are believed to have an excellent opportunity of going up in value in the short term and then selling them. Because this fund manager's investment style is to sell stocks with short-term gains, the profits earned will not be eligible for preferential long-term capital gain treatment.

Let's further assume that both Fund A and Fund B earn a 10 percent rate of return on the $100,000 investment, so each fund increases in value by $10,000 over the year. Of the 10 percent return for Fund A , 80 percent ($8,000) was attributed to growth in value of the stocks in the fund and 20 percent ($2,000) consisted of dividends that were paid out. Since Fund A was held in the IRA, the

$2,000 in dividends is not taxed and the value of Fund A at the end of the year is $110,000. Because the personal assets in Fund B were invested in a short-term trading strategy, the entire 10 percent return of $10,000 is fully taxable. If our hypothetical investor is in a 35 percent tax bracket, 35 percent of the $10,000 profit from Fund B ($3,500) is owed in taxes at the end of the year.

Table 9-1
Tax Inefficient Investing

Fund	A	B
Account	Tax-Deferred Account	Taxable Personal Funds
Strategy of Manager	Long-term	Short-term
Investment	$100,000	$100,000
Dividends	$2,000	0
Growth in Value	$8,000	0
Fund Distributions	0	$10,000
Fund Value at End of Year	$110,000	$110,000
Taxes @ 35 Percent	0	-$3,500
Net Value After Taxes	$110,000	$106,500
Combined Portfolio Value	$216,500	

But what if the investor had taken the time to examine the investment style of both funds before investing? Let's see what would occur if the investor reversed the funds. If the personal assets were invested in Fund A (the buy-and-hold fund) the investor would have to pay income taxes only on the $2,000 in dividends—a total of $700. If Fund B (with the $10,000 taxable distribution) were held inside the IRA, there would be no immediate income tax liability. Thus, it would be more tax efficient to invest the highly taxable Fund B within the IRA and to hold the less taxable Fund A personally, as shown in Table 9-2.

Table 9-2
Tax Efficient Investing

Fund	A	B
Account	Tax-Deferred Account	Taxable Personal Funds
Strategy of Manager	Short-term	Long-term
Investment	$100,000	$100,000
Dividends	0	$2,000
Growth in Value	0	$8,000
Fund Distributions	$10,000	0
Fund Value at End of Year	$110,000	$110,000
Taxes @ 35 Percent	0	-$700
Net Value After Taxes	$110,000	$109,300
Combined Portfolio Value	$219,300	

This example not only illustrates the importance of understanding the investment style of a prospective mutual fund or investment advisor, it also helps to identify the type of tax implications investors should explore before investing personal taxable assets or tax-deferred assets in 401(k)s, IRAs, or other qualified retirement plans.

In our example, equal amounts were invested in both the taxable and tax-deferred accounts. Even if this investor had a smaller amount invested in one account or another, he should not be discouraged from exploring whether he can make his portfolio more tax efficient.

LIFECYCLE INVESTING

When the subject of lifecycle investing comes up, most investors think of an age-based investment strategy recommending that the further you are from retirement, the larger the proportion of your portfolio that should be allocated to stocks. As you draw closer to retirement, the strategy advises you to reduce your portfolio's exposure to stocks (or other higher-risk investments). Upon retirement, you are advised to move to a more conservative portfolio that further reduces your percentage in stocks.

Because of its simplicity, lifecycle or age-based investing can cause investors to overlook important basic principles of investing. This could be dangerous. Let's create a hypothetical three-stage lifecyle model that addresses some critical issues. Suppose that in the first stage of his investment lifecycle, an investor allocates 80 percent of his portfolio to stocks and 20 percent to fixed-income investments; in the second stage he allocates 60 percent to stocks and 40 percent to fixed-income investments; and in retirement he allocates 20 percent to stocks and 80 percent to fixed-income investments. Let's also assume that the lifecycle spans 60 years, so each stage covers a 20-year period. Chart 9-3 summarizes this scenario.

Chart 9-3
Lifecycle Investing

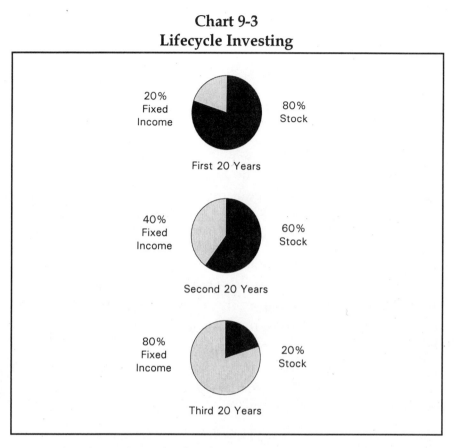

In this hypothetical, the first question an investor must ask himself is this: "Since the recommended allocation during the first stage is 80 percent in stocks, will I truly be comfortable with this level of volatility in my portfolio?" There is not necessarily a mathematical connection between age and an investor's ability to tolerate risk. Some younger investors will not be comfortable with the volatility of a portfolio with 80 percent in stocks, while some retired investors may be very comfortable with an allocation higher than 20 percent in stocks.

Our investor should also consider in advance whether he will rebalance his portfolio allocation throughout each stage. During the first stage, for example, 80 percent of the portfolio is allocated to stocks. Later, however, declining or increasing markets will cause the portfolio balance to change. If the portfolio is to be rebalanced to its original allocation, who is responsible for the rebalancing—the investor, an advisor, or a mutual fund manager?

Some investors feel that they can afford to take more portfolio risk when they are younger. While this may be true for some, others may be dealing with a period of unparalleled personal volatility in their lives (lack of job security, a troubled marriage, etc.) *Again we are reminded that personal volatility and statistical volatility must be considered together.*

Another important issue that lifecycle investors should consider is the implication of a large portion of their portfolios in stocks. Let's compare the returns of an investor who allocates 100 percent of his portfolio to stocks with those of an investor who allocates 80 percent to stocks and 20 percent to fixed-income investments. We will assume a 10 percent return for stocks and a 6 percent return for fixed-income. Table 9-3 illustrates the returns for these hypothetical portfolios.

Table 9-3
Returns of Portfolios with Differing Asset Allocations

100 Percent Stock Portfolio	80 Percent Stock/20 percent Fixed Income Portfolio
100% Stocks 10% Return = 10%	80% Stocks 10% Return =8.0% 20% Fixed Income 6% Return =1.2%
Total Portfolio Return = 10%	Total Portfolio Return =9.2%

An investor who chooses the 100 percent stock portfolio for its higher expected return must consider if it is worth giving up the potential benefits that may be achieved by diversifying the portfolio with fixed-income investments. The extra 0.8 percent return compounded annually could significantly increase the assets in an investor's portfolio given a long enough period of time. But the extra return may carry a big price tag: a higher level of volatility. Investors must weigh whether the increased risk of a less diversified portfolio is worth the hoped-for extra 0.8 percent return. *It is essential that this exercise be performed before making portfolio allocation decisions.*

Remember also, it is impossible to predict which lifecycle stage will produce the most favorable investment returns. What if the lowest returns for stocks are generated in the earliest stage, while the highest returns occur in the final 20-year stage? This could be a particularly difficult problem for investors who are following the conventional lifecyle strategy and investing most of their portfolio in stocks in the first stage. It is unlikely they will be able to meet their retirement goals.

Age, Confusion and History

In lifecycle investing, where a portfolio allocation is influenced by the age of the investor, it is easy to overlook the fact that there have been decades when bonds have outperformed stocks. There have also been 20-year periods (discussed in the Real Rates of Return chapter) when real rates of returns for large-company stocks averaged less than 2 percent per year. If stocks earn lower returns than expected, those who have allocated a significant portion of their portfolios to stocks could be in for a rude awakening. As noted earlier, investors who choose higher-risk investments receive no guarantee that they will be rewarded with higher returns.

The use of lifecycle or age-based portfolio allocations has increased in conjunction with the growth of 401(k) plans. Although this may be an appropriate investment strategy for some investors, it can be oversimplified. This can increase the chances that one or more important investment principles—such as personal volatility, diversification, or the true potential volatility of a portfolio's allocation—will be overlooked, at the investor's peril.

Summary: Tools for the Savvy Investor

- Understanding the limitations in computer programs used for retirement and investment decision-making can significantly increase your chances of using the software effectively.

- When using financial-based computer software, the most overlooked factor is the real-life personal volatility that can dramatically impact your frame of mind the day you use the program.

- If you dollar cost average, it is important to go through the mental exercise of picturing yourself continuing to invest your money even through prolonged declining markets.

- When you have a lump sum of money to invest, you must decide whether to invest it all at once or to do some form of dollar cost averaging. This issue is complex and requires careful psychological, cash flow, and other planning considerations.

- Once your portfolio is designed with a specific percentage allocated between equities and fixed-income investments, important criteria should be established in advance as to whether, how often, and on what basis to rebalance your portfolio.

- Tax-efficient investing of personal assets and retirement plan assets can afford opportunities for you to minimize income taxes on your portfolio.

- If you use age-based or lifecycle investing, don't overlook the critical planning issues of risk, volatility and diversification.

AUTHOR'S CONCERNS AND OBSERVATIONS

Throughout this book we have not only examined important investment principles, but also discussed the difficulties and complexities of investing when most of us will be investors for 20 to 50 years. We also discussed how the challenge becomes even more complicated when investors consider the impact of both the technological revolution and the personal changes and volatility that we will all encounter over the course of their lives.

In this last chapter of this book I want to relate some personal experiences that illustrate my concerns about how we can unwittingly overlook important investment principles, and often be seduced into accepting simple solutions to complex problems. I also want to share some observations on other issues investors may overlook that could be crucial to their long-term planning.

SOME PERSONAL EXPERIENCES

Risk and Long-term Projections

Most investors I meet feel they have an excellent understanding of the risks they are taking when they invest. However, I have found that it is quite easy for these same investors to overlook investment risk when it comes to doing financial planning.

I was recently asked to advise the managing partner of a large consulting firm who was responsible for overseeing 500 consultants. He is 57 years old and wants to retire at age 62. In planning for his retirement, he told me he would have adequate assets to provide a comfortable retirement income, and thought he was using a conservative estimate of expected return on his investments. His portfolio was invested in a combination of fixed income investments and stocks. This investor mentioned that he had considered investing in all risk-free investments but concluded they would not provide high enough returns to accumulate the assets he needed to retire.

I asked him, "Did you ever consider the possibility that in five years your investments could be worth the same as they are today, or perhaps even less?" He replied with some irritation: "No, because if that occurred, I wouldn't have enough money to retire."

Let's examine some of the reasons for his irritation. After spending considerable time planning for his retirement and using conservative assumptions, he had projected that he could retire at his desired age. He was excited about the prospect of a retirement where he could finally pursue those hobbies and interests he never had the time for now. The idea that his portfolio would not increase in value—let alone the possibility of losing money—was something he had not considered.

This investor had very little experience with assets declining in value because most of his investments had been made after the bear market of 1973-1974. He had seen a significant short-term decline during the fourth quarter 1987 stock market crash, but like the overall market, his portfolio finished up in value for the year. My conversation with this investor reminded me how vulnerable any one can become to financial projections. He was subconsciously *ignoring the existence of risk*, by not even acknowledging the possibility that between now and his projected retirement age his assets would not continue to grow in value.

The retirement projections had lulled him into thinking and believing that his assets were going to grow just as he anticipated. This state of mind can blind us to the danger of being unprepared for market reversals, whether short or long term. The idea of only positive outcomes is often the result of our exposure to financial literature and promotional materials. Seldom, if ever, do we see charts, graphs, or educational information that project our investments could be worth less in the future.

Some investors may use the same projected return from today through retirement while others may assume a higher pre-retirement return and a lower one post-retirement. Yet, both approaches are based on a future where their investments are *always growing in value*. Constantly holding to the belief in increasing values subtly encourages investors to feel that their assets are not at risk—which is a very dangerous perception. Such projections are just one of the reasons many investors are unprepared and often shocked when their assets decline in value.

Expected Versus Actual Returns — A Potential Retirement Disaster

Many individuals are relying on dangerous assumptions in their retirement planning because they have not considered the impact of portfolio withdrawals in years when their investment return is *less* than was projected.

For example, an individual investor estimates that a compound return of 8 percent will provide the spending level he needs during retirement. But we know that in the real world, the investor will not receive a constant 8 percent rate of return year after year. Yet, in each year of retirement, no matter what the investment return, he still needs to withdraw money to live on. In years when the actual returns are less than the expected returns and withdrawals are made, the future value of the portfolio can be significantly impacted. If lower returns come during the early years of retirement, the individual will run out of money even if the overall projected rate of 8 percent is met! The same problem exists regardless of what projected rate is used.

What actually occurs is the opposite of dollar cost averaging where more of the portfolio is liquidated during down years, as opposed to buying more shares of stocks during down years. As a result, many retirees may find themselves running out of money during retirement.

Since this investor did not consider the idea that his projections might not be met, he also didn't think about any contingency planning. The investor believed that not meeting his retirement projections left him with only one distasteful option—not being able to retire at his desired age. For him, the future was black and white:

he either would have enough money to retire or not. But other possibilities exist; just like other areas of our lives, the answers may be in shades of gray. For example, this investor might consider deferring retirement for a few more years, or working part time for a number of years before a complete retirement. He could also consider reducing his spending during retirement, or increase his pre-retirement savings rate, or some combination of these variables.

This type of contingency planning can accomplish two objectives: help him plan for what he will do if his projections are not met; and serve as an important reminder of the ever-present existence of risk.

Experiencing a Down Market

Often I meet with investors who believe they have a very clear idea of how they would react to down markets. However, actually dealing with down markets may be far more difficult than many of them imagine.

One day I received a phone call from an investor who had some questions regarding retirement planning. The caller was a professional whose work required both precision and discipline. He told me that he was a seasoned investor with over 20 years of generally favorable investment experiences; he had seen his assets significantly increase in value over this period. I asked what he would do with his portfolio if markets significantly declined in value. He immediately answered: "I would welcome a down market because it would give me an excellent opportunity to buy more stock at a lower price." Given his background and the knowledge he demonstrated in our conversation, I had the distinct impression that he had a firm understanding of his investment strategy.

But when this investor called me three months later, during a week when the market had gone down almost 5 percent, he told me he was getting very nervous about his portfolio because of the decline. I reminded him that historically, on average, the market has produced negative returns about 1 of every 5 months over the past 71 years, so it was not unusual nor unexpected.

After our conversation I thought, "What would his reaction have been if the market had declined more severely? If he is upset with a one-week decline in the market, how will he react to a long-term decline over many months or possibly years?" This was the same person who had clearly stated earlier that he would "welcome" the buying opportunity of a down market!

This incident illustrates that we can think we are going to act a certain way, but when tested we often act very differently. Here was a seasoned investor, from a disciplined and exacting profession, who thought it would be easy to apply similar discipline and a non-emotional attitude to his investment decisions.

When I talk with other investors about how they might react to down markets I am reminded of this experience. The overwhelming majority feel confident they can weather poor markets. Many investors convey this belief in their answers on risk-tolerance questionnaires and in interviews. Common responses include: "I know if I just hold on for 20 years I can't lose in the stock market;" "I didn't panic during the Crash of 1987;" "I fully understand that markets are volatile and it won't bother me;" "My stocks won't be affected by a market decline."

I don't question the sincerity of these investors. However, when I attempt to point out that investing may actually be much more difficult over the long run than they think, many individuals become uncomfortable or even irritated. If I pursue the discussion further, they may even think I am questioning their integrity or beliefs. Investors truly believe they have the personality traits and discipline, or the investment knowledge, necessary to endure prolonged market declines. However, history has shown that most have acted otherwise.

It is difficult to fully understand something we have not experienced first-hand. You may go on a vacation and bring back photographs of a sunset, or a great cathedral. You may capture your children in a special moment. You can excitedly share your pictures with friends and relatives and try to express the feelings you had when you took the photograph. But regardless of how clearly we describe the situation and our feelings about it, others cannot completely share the experience the same way we did because they were not personally involved in it. In a similar way, many investors have not experienced significant investment losses, and particularly have not had the first-hand experience of a prolonged down market where their portfolios showed a steady erosion in value month by month over long periods of time.

Our experienced investor's emotional reaction to a one-week market decline demonstrates that the way an investor *thinks* he will react to a down market can be the opposite of how he *actually reacts* to it. Investors may intellectually perceive they are prepared for the possibility of a long down market and some may even think they know how they will react if one occurs. However, the real question is: *do you have a chance of not reacting emotionally without having had the first-hand, real-life experience of going through a prolonged down market?* Understanding this sobering fact can help make you a better investor.

The Role of Personal Volatility

The unique personal circumstances faced by any particular investor can have an enormous impact on his or her ability to tolerate portfolio risk. It is essential to consider such factors when formulating a long-term investment policy.

A graphic reminder of this issue surfaced when I met with an individual who was in the profession of educating and advising other investors. This advisor had a background in finance, law and accounting. He worked at a large accounting firm and was the head of their financial planning division. In advising both individuals and groups, he generally recommended that investors with investment time horizons of 20 or more years should consider investing 100 percent of their portfolios in stocks.

I asked whether he believed a portfolio invested 100 percent in stocks was more volatile than most investors could tolerate. He answered, "Absolutely not," saying that he was 40 years old and had 100 percent of his own assets invested in a diversified portfolio of stocks.

I then asked him how secure he was in his job, and he replied: "Not very—my profession doesn't provide near the security it once did." My next question was: "What would happen to your investment strategy if you lost your job?" He answered: "I could never stay with a strategy of 100 percent in stocks. I could not tolerate that kind of volatility in my portfolio if I was out of work."

I could see that as he listened to his own answers to my questions, he was startled. Upon reflection, he told me that when he designed his portfolio he had not considered the impact that losing his job or other personal circumstances might have on his investment choices. He acknowledged these non-financial issues could change the way he invested his money *even though* he still had a long investment time horizon.

It is important to consider the potential impact job security or other personal circumstances can have on your investment choices.

OTHER OBSERVATIONS

Contingency Planning

At some point, investors have to address the issue of their own diminished physical or mental capacity, particularly in post-retirement years. Some may have trouble dealing with important investment issues because of an inability to think clearly or quickly due to impaired reasoning or shorter attention spans. An older person might have a stroke or Alzheimer's disease, or just become more forgetful. Unfortunately, even during these difficult times, the need to make essential investment decisions will not go away.

It is therefore critical that all investors prepare for such a contingency. Proper legal documentation should establish who will be responsible for making financial decisions when difficulties occur. If the investor is married, the spouse should not automatically be placed in the decision-making role. A spouse may not have the necessary background or desire to take on greater responsibility for investment decisions simultaneously with increased day-to-day decision-making and care.

Many investors have gone to great lengths to find a qualified investment advisor yet have failed to establish a legal method for continuing that relationship in event of incapacity. All investors should consider preparing some kind of contingency plan for their financial matters.

Perceptions of Losses

I've had many conversations demonstrating that people tend to focus more on *what they feel they have lost* as opposed to *what they have actually gained*. Suppose a couple buys a house for $50,000 that subsequently increases in value to $150,000. Then economic conditions change, causing the house to drop to $110,000. When this occurs the couple only focuses on the fact that they had a house that was once worth $150,000 but is now worth $110,000. They say, "We have lost $40,000!" This is their perception, even though they originally paid $50,000 for the house and *it has increased $60,000 in value since they purchased it.* The majority of people will only look at the recent amount they perceive to have lost and not the overall increase in value.

The same thing happens with investors who have seen their portfolios grow over time and then decline in value. They experience the same psychological reaction, they say: "My portfolio went from $200,000 to $300,000 and then down to $250,000. I've lost $50,000!" not "My portfolio has increased $50,000 since I started." Once we have emotionally experienced an increase in portfolio value, we feel that it's what we deserve to keep—that we have earned it. If there is a later decrease in value, we feel that *something has been taken away from us.*

Investors who have the mental discipline to focus on the gain in an investment and not on the perceived loss can increase their chances of surviving normal market volatility. They will also be less inclined to let their emotions dictate their investment policy.

Underestimating Retirement Needs

Many investors are unaware that they face a severe financial burden regarding their retirement health care. By the year 2012, there will be over 70 million people on Medicare—a system that is financially doomed without radical changes. Regardless of what Congress may do in the short term, at some point in the future it will be necessary to implement some form of severe rationing of Medicare services, and those services will be far different from what they are today.

Medicare recipients who want the highest level of medical care with the most advanced technology available, particularly in the latter years of their lives, may have to pay for a large part of that care out of their own pockets. Since many investors have not factored the cost of such medical needs into their retirement projections, they may be underestimating the assets that may be required for their future. Thus, it will be important for you to build a contingency reserve for medical care into your retirement planning.

How Technology Speeds the Decision-Making Process

Because of technology and the information revolution, we now have to make decisions, even very important ones, faster than ever before. As a result, we have less time for reflective thinking. While some of the decisions we are forced to make quickly are easy, others can be quite subtle and difficult.

A friend of mine is a lawyer who specializes in drafting contracts. He used to receive contracts in the mail to review, and then mail them back to his clients with suggested changes. They would go back and forth by mail until a contract was finalized. With the onset of express mail services, his clients began sending the contracts overnight, and they now expected them to be worked on and returned the following day. Next, fax machines entered the picture. Contracts were faxed in the morning, and clients expected them to be reviewed and faxed back by the end of the day.

In order to satisfy the client's demands, my friend adapted to the technology. But the speed at which that technology allowed him to serve his clients also gave him less time for reflective thinking. As a result of working at a faster pace, he worried that he might be making mistakes, missing important issues, or not having the time to think of more creative solutions to his clients' problems.

A computer now allows us to perform tasks in ten minutes that might have taken two hours in the past. And what is being done with that extra hour and 50 minutes of time? Are people working less or spending more free time with family and friends, or on hobbies? Or, as a result of the time that technology has "saved" them, are they expected to get even more work completed in less time?

The pace at which technology has advanced in many fields has created a new workplace where everyone attempts to produce more work at a faster and faster pace every year. In essence, this is no different than the situation faced by factory workers during the industrial revolution.

While the information revolution is giving us nearly instantaneous information, it can also induce us to make hasty decisions. Unfortunately, when it comes to investing, snap judgments made without reflective thinking often result in inappropriate decisions.

Today's Stresses Compounded by a Down Market

There are tens of millions of people today whose ability to retire or attain other essential financial goals is dependent on the performance of their investments. Because of this, it is quite possible we could see widespread investor panic, if we face a prolonged down market such as the one in 1973-74.

Today's investors are much more vulnerable to reacting hastily to declining markets. Employers have either eliminated or de-emphasized traditional pension plans which provided employees with a guaranteed retirement income for life without any contribution or investment responsibility. As employers started to adopt 401(k) plans and other types of self-directed retirement plans, a significant shift occurred. Many employees are now responsible not only for saving the assets they need to retire, but also for making the investment decisions about how to invest those retirement assets. The investment performance of 401(k)s, IRAs or other self-directed retirement accounts may dictate whether these employees will have the necessary assets for a comfortable retirement.

Anxiety over future financial security may spill over into the workplace where it can impact job productivity and create problems for employers. The trauma caused by a prolonged down market may have a domino effect when we consider the fact that many employees already have the stress of diminished job security. In addition, the enormous influence of the media reporting primarily negative news, in a society where information is disseminated so rapidly, creates an environment where any prolonged down market can take an enormous financial and psychological toll on investors.

The responsibility and stress of investing will not go away. However, if you recognize the kind of psychological toll and demands you may have to face someday, you will increase the chance that your emotions will not dictate your investment policy.

Reminders of Other Losses

Throughout this book we have discussed the important role of investor behavior and its impact on investing. If investors see their assets significantly decline in value it is human nature to be disappointed, frustrated, or maybe even angry.

However, there is another aspect of human nature that is often involved in the investment process. In order to cope with losses and painful experiences we may have encountered during our lives, it is not unusual to suppress feelings about them. An investor may have recovered from a divorce, loss of a loved one, difficulties in childhood or other painful experiences but incurring financial losses may stir up reminders. If he sees his assets decline in value, it can trigger emotions from those other losses that may cause him to react more intensely than other investors. Experiencing a financial decline can cause you to relive old fears, insecurities and anxieties unless you are prepared for it in advance.

The Danger of Feeling Invincible

Most individuals have some part of their lives where they are consistently successful. This could be achievements at work or success in leisure activities such as music, sports, card games, or gardening. When we are very good at what we do, particularly over extended periods of time, it's natural to develop a feeling of confidence and invincibility. This creates a frame of mind where we expect our successes to continue in the future.

But when it comes to investing, feeling invincible can be dangerous. *It can lead investors to overlook the principles that significantly contributed to their success in the first place.* Feeling invincible can cause investors to act as if their investments are guaranteed winners. It may be helpful to point out past examples where others felt their investments were a "sure thing."

In the late 1970s and early 1980s, real estate tax shelter partnerships "guaranteed" investment success through a combination of tax write-offs and increasing property values. Investors felt so invincible about these investments that they ignored fundamental investment principles. Many of these partnerships eventually went bankrupt because of overbuilding, high interest rates, a severe recession and unexpected changes in the tax law. As a result, many individual suffered significant financial losses in these "can't lose" investments.

A feeling of invincibility can also affect investors in the stock market. For example, in late 1960s and early 1970s there was a group of blue-chip stocks called the "Nifty Fifty." These stocks were the favorites of sophisticated institutional money managers who selected investments for large pension funds, endowments and other large pools of money. The Nifty Fifty had stellar records of growth and stability and were widely held because of their perceived ability to weather poor markets. Then the prolonged down stock market of 1973 and 1974 caused the Nifty Fifty to lose a staggering 80 percent of its collective value. Some professionals who previously felt invincible about their stock picks lost confidence and abandoned their long-term investment strategies. Some even left the market altogether.

Investors who feel invincible should remind themselves that as recently as the 20-year period ending in 1981, if they had 100 percent of their portfolios in the S&P 500, they would have received *less than a 1 percent average annual compound return over inflation* during that 20-year period. They should also remind themselves that after the Dow Jones Industrial Average peaked in 1968, it declined and didn't reach that peak again *until 14 years later* in 1982.

When you start to feel invincible, which is easy to do when investments steadily increase in value over extended periods, you can easily overlook investment fundamentals. This oversight can result in poor investment decisions.

Close

It is my hope that you will never lose sight of the Terrible Truths we have discussed as you attempt to achieve your long-term investment goals. Consider this book not only as an introduction, but also an ongoing guide—a source you can turn to throughout your investment life for answers to the questions that will arise continuously as you invest.

Your dreams and goals for the future are tremendously important—not only to you but to all the people whose lives you touch. To achieve those goals, you need to be well versed in fundamental investment principles. If you fully understand the *Terrible Truths About Investing*, you will be able to make better financial and investment decisions. I believe these Terrible Truths are tools that can help when you are confronted by the challenges that await you. While it is true that investing is complex, relying on these fundamental truths can make it more manageable.

Perhaps more importantly, you will be a better investor if you integrate your own unique personal life experiences into your investment and financial decision-making. You need to be aware of the pitfalls of reacting emotionally to the normal uncertainty and unpredictability of markets, as well as the impact that the successes and difficulties you will experience in your career and personal life can have on your investing. *Only by integrating the personal with the financial can you truly become a savvy investor.*

GLOSSARY

Active Management An approach to investing where managers believe they can exercise their skill to beat the investment returns of the market indexes. Active money managers may use fundamental analysis of individual stocks, technical analysis of past trends of groups of stocks, market timing or other methods of selecting investments.

Actuarial Table A statistical table primarily used by insurance companies which shows average life expectancies.

After-Tax Return The net return on an investment after taxes have been deducted from the investment's gross return.

American Stock Exchange (AMEX) A stock exchange second only in size to the New York Stock Exchange. The AMEX lists 700 stocks, most of which are smaller in market value than those listed on the New York Stock Exchange (NYSE).

Annuity An investment contract, usually issued by an insurance company that can provide a fixed income for life. There are different types of investment annuities, some of which begin payments immediately and others which allow income to accumulate tax-deferred until a future date. *See* Variable Annuity.

Appreciation The term used to describe the increase in value of a stock, bond or other asset over its original purchase price. Part of the total return of an investment.

Asset Anything owned that has value.

Asset Allocation   The process of dividing a portfolio's investments among various asset classes in accordance with an investor's risk tolerance, target rate of return and financial goals. This term can also refer to an investment style of a mutual fund. *See* Portfolio Design.

Asset Class   A category of investment assets which has common risk and return characteristics. Typical asset classes include large-company U.S. stocks, small-company U.S. stocks, international stocks, corporate bonds, government bonds, real estate, cash, or precious metals such as gold.

Average Return   The sum of the return for each time period divided by the number of time periods. This is also known as "simple average return." For example, if the return on an investment for 1994 was 5 percent, for 1995 was 10 percent, and for 1996 was 15 percent, its simple average annual return over this three-year period would be 10 percent (5 plus 10 plus 15=30 divided by 3=10). *See* Geometric Return.

Baby Boomer/Baby Boom Generation   The group of children born in America after World War II from 1946 through 1964. This group, consisting of 77 million people, has produced an unprecedented demographic "bulge" in American society because of the enormity of its size.

Balanced Fund   A mutual fund that has two investment objectives: current income and capital growth. A balanced fund generally invests in both stocks and bonds in attempting to meet its investment objectives.

Basis   The initial cost of an investment. The "cost basis" is used to determine whether an investment has a taxable gain or loss when sold by the investor. For example, if an investor buys a share of stock for $20 and then sells it for $30, $20 is the "basis," and the gain is $10. Basis in a mutual fund will include all purchases of shares and any reinvested dividends.

Bear Market   A market that declines in value over a period of time. Although there is no common definition of a bear market, many investment professionals would say that three successive calendar quarters of negative market returns, or an overall drop of 20 percent, would constitute a bear market.

Blue Chip A nickname for the common stock of large, well-known companies with a relatively stable record of earnings and dividend payouts over a long period of time. General Electric and Coca-Cola are examples of blue chip companies. This term is thought to originate from poker, where the blue chips are the most valuable.

Bond A debt investment where one party (a lender) lends money to another party (a borrower). Bonds are issued by corporations, development projects and governmental entities. Investors who buy bonds lend money at a fixed rate of interest (usually paid in semi-annual payments) for a stated period of time. Once that period of time is up (on the "maturity date") the principal (the original amount of money lent to the borrower) will be paid back. Note: corporate bonds have "default" risk which is the risk of the borrower going bankrupt and not repaying interest and principal to bondholders. This risk is why corporate bonds often pay higher rates of interest than government bonds (which do not have a default risk). In addition, most corporate and government bonds can be repaid before the bond's maturity date, at a "call date." *See* Fixed Income.

Bond Funds Mutual funds which invest in a variety of bonds. Bond funds seek maximization of income rather than growth of investment capital. Unlike individual bonds, most bond funds have no fixed maturity date.

Book Value The total assets of a company (as shown on their financial records or "books") minus its liabilities. This method generally understates a company's value because the company's assets are often stated on its books at historic values (i.e., the original purchase prices paid by the company for the assets) rather than current or appreciated value.

Bull Market A market that is going up in value. One of the most sustained bull markets of the Twentieth century occurred in the 1980s, when stock markets were up for 9 out of 10 years and the average annual compound return of the S&P 500 Index was 17.5%.

Buy and Hold Buying and holding investments for the long term rather than doing a lot of buying and selling. Followers of this strategy tend to ignore both up and down market fluctuations, regardless of how severe, and remain invested in the market at all times.

Capital Gain A capital gain is the profit from the sale of certain assets. Under current law the gains from an investment that has been held for 12 months or more (called "long-term gains") are taxed at a lower rate than other forms of income.

Capital Gains Distribution When a mutual fund sells assets it may realize a capital gain. These capital gains are then passed through or "distributed" to the fund's investors as capital gain distributions and the investors pay taxes on the gains.

Cash Equivalents Money invested in short-term savings accounts, money market funds, and Treasury bills are considered to be "cash equivalents" because the values are very stable and easily converted to cash.

Certificate of Deposit A certificate from a bank or savings and loan documenting receipt of money to be held for a specified period of time at a predetermined rate of interest (a loan to the bank). Some are negotiable (sold on the secondary market) and others are not. *See* Fixed Income.

Common Stock An asset which represents a share of ownership in a corporation and a portion of the profits in the form of dividends. Also called "equities." Stock investors risk losses if stock prices decline or if the stocks become worthless. However, they can profit if stock prices increase. *See* Equities.

Compound Interest The payment of interest on previously earned interest. For example, you open an account with a certain amount of money and then earn interest on that money (called "principal"). As time passes, interest is earned not only on the original principal, but also on the interest already earned which creates a compounding effect. The greater the number of compounding intervals, whether daily monthly, quarterly, semi-annually or annually, and the higher the interest rate, the greater the total interest earned.

Compound Return Investment returns that are calculated on the original amount of money invested, plus (or minus) the periodic increase (or decrease) in its value, plus the total interest or dividends received over a period of time. Usually expressed as an annualized number.

Consumer Price Index (CPI) An index published monthly by the Labor Department. The CPI is a measure of inflation at the consumer level that is designed to reflect changes in the cost of living. This is done by calculating average retail prices for a basket of consumer goods and services on an annual basis. The government has changed how it determines the CPI on numerous occasions.

Corporate Bond A fixed-income or debt investment issued by a corporation. *See* Bond, Fixed income.

Cost of Living Adjustment (COLA) A provision in collective bargaining agreements, private contracts or government plans (such as pensions and Social Security) whereby benefits are regularly adjusted to reflect increases in the inflation rate.

Cross Correlation The attempt to mathematically quantify patterns of returns in different asset classes or investments and relate them to one another. Two assets that move in different directions from each other over the same period of time are said to be negatively correlated; assets that move in a similar pattern are positively correlated.

Debt Instrument Evidence of ownership of a debt in which the investor has loaned money and expects to be repaid. Corporate and government bonds, municipal bonds, certificates of deposit and Treasury bills are examples of debt instruments. *See* Bond, Fixed Income.

Default Risk The possibility that a bond issuer will default and fail to pay principal or interest to a bondholder in a timely manner (or at all). Corporate "junk" bonds typically have the highest possibility of default, hence feature the highest yields to induce the investor to take the extra risk.

Defined Benefit Pension Plan A type of pension plan offered by some employers which provides a monthly income for life, usually when the employee retires. Generally, employees do not contribute to these plans or have responsibility for making any investment decisions. Most defined benefit plans have limited or no cost of living adjustments (COLAs).

Deflation This is the opposite of inflation. Deflation results in decreasing prices while inflation produces increasing prices. In a deflationary environment, one dollar will purchase more today than it did yesterday, whereas in inflationary times it will purchase less today than it did yesterday. Deflation has not occurred in the U.S. since 1954. *See* Inflation.

Diversification The process of spreading out money among different investments in an attempt to reduce risk or volatility or increase returns.

Dividends The payment of a company's earnings, that is proportionately distributed to its shareholders according to the number of shares of common stock held by them.

Dollar Cost Averaging A system of making investments at regular intervals with a fixed amount of money. Investors using this approach can obtain an average cost per share that is lower or higher than if they had purchased the shares all at once. This system helps investors buy fewer shares when prices are high and more shares when prices are low. However, dollar-cost averaging is not a guarantee investors can avoid a loss or earn a profit.

Dow Jones Industrial Average The most well-known stock market performance indicator in the world. The Dow-Jones Industrial Average (the "Dow") is comprised of stocks in 30 "blue chip" companies such as Coca-Cola, General Electric and DuPont. *See* complete list on page 28 of Chapter 2.

Emerging Markets These are investments in stock markets of newly emerging second- and third-tier countries in the regions of the Far East, Africa, Europe, Central and South America.

Equities Stocks in a company or some other evidence of ownership, such as real estate or a business venture. As an owner, you participate in the fortunes—good and bad—of the entity you have invested in.

Expense Ratio The proportion of a mutual fund's total annual operating expenses expressed as a percentage of its average net assets. Some of the expenses reflected in this ratio include investment advisory fees, administrative fees, record-keeping expenses and marketing expenses. However, commissions, trading costs and taxes are not included in this ratio. The annual operating expenses charged to investors by the average stock mutual fund are approximately 1.50 percent per year. However, expense ratios can range from 0.2 percent per year for an index fund to close to 3 percent for some mutual funds.

Fixed-Income Lending money through bonds, certificates of deposit, etc., that pay a fixed amount of interest. Note that the value of certain fixed income investments can fluctuate in value, because of fluctuations in interest rates and other factors. Changes in the values of bonds at times can be even more volatile than the change in value in stocks.

Fundamental Analysis A method of evaluating a company in an attempt to establish an accurate estimate of its "true" value. *See* p. 188.

Genetic Profile The health and longevity history of an individual's immediate family and other close relatives. This can be an extremely important factor in how an investor goes about setting up his or her investment strategy for retirement and other long term goals.

Geometric Return A method of calculating returns which links investment results on a periodic basis and thus recognizes the effect of compounding in the return calculation. Suppose a $100 investment returned 25% in the first quarter (producing an ending value of $125), but lost 20% in the second quarter (ending value is $100). Over the two quarters, the geometric return would be 0% because the beginning and ending value are both $100. *See* Arithmetic Return.

Global Fund A mutual fund which includes investments in both U.S. and international markets. Such funds could hold either fixed income or stock investments.

Government Securities Bonds issued and backed by the "full faith and credit" of the United States government. These securities include Treasury bills, Treasury notes and bonds of different maturities and are considered among the safest investments in the financial markets. May also include debt instruments issued by government agencies, such as GNMA.

Guaranteed Investment Contract (GIC) A debt instrument offered to investors by insurance companies that guarantees a fixed interest rate for a particular period of time, similar to a bond. *See* Bond, Debt Instrument, Fixed Income.

Holding Period The length of time an investment is held by an investor.

Index A group of stocks, bonds or other securities that has been selected to measure and reflect the investment performance of a particular asset class that makes up a segment of a financial market. Many indexes are published daily. The index considered to be the most representative of "the market" is the S&P 500 Index.

Index Fund A mutual fund that attempts to provide the performance of a specific index by holding all the assets that are represented in the index. An index fund does not attempt to "beat the market" but only to match its performance. For example, the Vanguard S&P 500 index mutual fund seeks to match the performance of the S&P 500 Index. Index funds are not actively managed and often have very low expense ratios.

Inflation A persistent rise in prices so that the things that you buy today will cost more in the future. When inflation occurs, the purchasing power of a dollar will decline over time as prices rise. *See* Deflation.

Inflation-Adjusted The process of reducing an investment rate of return by the rate of inflation or increasing an annuity calculation to include a rate of inflation, in order to protect the purchasing power of an income stream.

Inflation Risk The possibility that inflation will so erode the purchasing power of an investor's savings that he or she will not be able to maintain his or her standard of living. The risk that things will cost more in the future than they do today.

Institutional Investor Investment entities whose primary purpose is to invest assets held in trust for others. Examples of institutional investors include pension plans, mutual funds, endowment funds for universities, insurance companies, banks, charitable organizations and other entities.

Interest The money paid by a borrower to a lender for the use of his or her money. For example, the money paid as income on a bond or certificate of deposit is paid in the form of interest.

Interest Rate Risk The uncertainty of the return on a bond caused by changes in its value due to changes in interest rates. These changes can be caused by shifts in inflation, creditworthiness, interest rates and general economic conditions. The longer a bond's maturity, the more its price will fluctuate for a given interest rate movement. Thus, a 5-year bond will not be as subject to as much interest rate risk as a 20-year bond of the same quality simply because the longer bond has to undergo the risk of an additional 15 years of fluctuations in interst rates.

Intermediate-term Bonds Bonds that are generally defined to have maturities of two to ten years.

International Fund A mutual fund that invests in foreign securities not traded on stock exchanges in the United States. Because foreign stock markets impose high trading and other costs, international mutual funds typically have higher annual operating expenses. In contrast, "global" mutual funds invest in both U.S. and international securities.

Investment Advisor An individual or organization that manages an

THE TERRIBLE TRUTH ABOUT INVESTING

investment portfolio and makes day-to-day investment decisions regarding the purchase and/or sale of investments. Some investment advisors are paid on a fee-only basis while others receive commissions on the purchase and/or sale of investment products sold to their investor-clients.

Investment Style A certain approach to investing taken by an investor such as picking "growth" stocks or "value" stocks. Different investment styles produce varying results in markets over the same time periods. For example, sometimes growth stocks achieve better returns than value stocks and vice versa. Many money managers defy clear-cut categorization and use elements of more than one investment style. Some styles are:

a. **allocators** managers who divide a portfolio between stocks, bonds and cash according to their prediction of which asset classes will perform well in the future.

b. **balanced** managers who mix stocks and bonds in an effort to obtain relatively greater stability of both principal and income. Generally, this involves a three-part investment objective (1) conservation of investment capital, (2) payment of current income and (3) maximization of income and capital.

c. **bottom-up** managers who start the analytical process by first looking at consumer trends and other basic economic preferences and then finding companies that benefit from those preferences.

d. **contrarians** those whose approach is to do the opposite of what the majority of other investors are doing at any given time. Contrarians seek to find value where no one else is looking by purchasing securities in unpopular or unconventional asset classes or industries.

e. **core** managers who purchase securities which represent basic and important companies and industries at the core of the economy.

f. **growth** those who seek stocks that are predicted to return profits at a greater annual rate than average. Aggressive growth managers desire maximum capital gains and do not worry about current income.

g. **index** stock and bond funds who purchase and sell investments in order to match the composition and thus provide the performance of an index. Also called "passive."

h. **price-driven** those managers to whom the price of a stock is the most important criterion.

i. **rotators** managers who move money between market sectors or industries attempting to be in the right place at the right time.

j. **market timers** those who attempt to forecast market movements in order to buy low and sell high. Used for both stocks and bonds.

k. **top-down** managers who approach analysis from the top (national policy and the economy) to find stocks that will benefit from current macroeconomic trends.

l. **value** those who select stocks based on today's relative value. An "undervalued" stock is defined as one that is worth intrinsically more than its current market price. Value investors are bargain hunters who attempt to buy stocks that they believe are currently selling below their "true" underlying investment value.

m. **yield** managers who seek securities (stocks or bonds) that have high dividend or interest income.

Investment Time Horizon The length of time that an individual has his or her money invested for a particular investment goal.

Joint Life Expectancy The oldest average age that one or the other of a couple is expected to live according to life insurance company actuarial tables. For example, the joint current average life expectancy of a healthy 65-year old couple is 88 years, which means that one of the persons would have a 50% chance of living to this age.

Large-company Stocks An asset class of stocks that includes companies with large market capitalization. The large-company asset class represents about 65-75% of the total market value of all stocks listed in

United States stock markets. The investment performance of this asset class is measured by the Standard & Poor's 500 stock index (S&P 500) or The Dow Jones Industrial Index (Dow). Large-company stocks are also known as "blue chip" or "large cap" stocks. As of the end of 1996, the market value of the smallest stock in the S&P 500 was approximately $190 million. Other stocks in the S&P 500 have market values in the tens of billions of dollars.

Lender An entity, whether individual or corporate, that lends money to others through fixed-income or debt investments such as bonds, certificates of deposits, guaranteed investment contracts or Treasury bills. *See* Bond.

Lifecycle Investing An investment strategy based on the idea that investors should invest more "aggressively" when they are young and more "conservatively" when they get older. "Aggressive investments" are usually thought of as stocks while "conservative investments" are fixed-income investments such as bonds.

Life Expectancy The average expected future lifetime for people at a particular age according to a mortality table. This average is based on looking at statistics for a large group of people. "Average" means that some people will die prior to the actuarial life expectancy and some people will die after the actuarial life expectancy. "Expectancy" depends on a person's current age, and will increase as a person grows older. For example, a 45-year old female has a life expectancy of 33.88 years, or attained age of 78.88 while a 65-year old female has an expectancy of 17.32 years, or attained age of 82.32. Life expectancy figures frequently quoted in the media are recorded from birth and usually are U.S. population statistics. Life expectancies will also differ depending on the chosen mortality table.

Liquidity How quickly an investment can be converted into cash with very little shrinkage in value. *See* Marketability.

Long Term A phrase that is often used but seldom quantified—as in "I am a long-term investor." It means different things to different people. For example, the investment media often defines long term as a five-year period of time. For fixed-income investments, long term implies maturities of more than 10 years.

Long-term Bonds Bonds that are generally defined to have maturities of greater than ten years. Beginning in 1977, the U.S. government began issuing 30-year Treasury bonds, which are now considered the benchmark for long-term government bonds.

Market Capitalization The "market value" of a company's stock. It is the current price of the stock multiplied by the total number of shares of the stock held by investors. Suppose that a share of stock of Bedrock Industries has a current market price of $28 per share and that investors hold a total of one million shares of Bedrock Industries stock. The total market capitalization (value) of Bedrock Industries stock would be $28 million.

Market Cycle The distance from peak to peak or trough to trough of a cycle in the stock market. A market cycle can only be seen in hindsight; it is virtually impossible to identify at the time of its occurrence.

Market Risk That portion of total investment risk that is inherent in a financial market such as the stock or bond market that cannot be diversified away or eliminated. This kind of risk is also known as "non-diversifiable" risk. It is the risk that an investor must bear for remaining invested in any financial market. The only way that this kind of risk can be avoided is to invest only in "risk-free" Treasury bills or other cash equivalents.

Market Timing an investment strategy based on the idea that it is possible to accurately predict the up and down market price movements of stocks and bonds. The goal of a market timer is to buy asset classes before they go up in value and to sell them before they go down in value.

Marketability This refers to the degree of ease with which an investment can be converted to cash, whether or not there is a loss of value as a result. Large company stocks, government securities and investment quality bonds can be readily sold in the open market so they are very marketable. Note that marketability does not guarantee an investor will sell the asset for the original purchase price or current value, just the ease at which it can be sold. "Thinly traded" stocks, in contrast, may not be as marketable. *See* Liquidity.

Maturity Date The date on which a bond's principal is to be repaid to the bondholder. For example, a 20-year U.S. Treasury bond issued in February 1997 might have a maturity date of February 15, 2017, at which time the government would pay off the bond. *See* Bond.

Modern Portfolio Theory This theory shows how an investor can estimate, manage and control investment risk and thereby relative expected investment return by properly diversifying a portfolio. This investment approach changes the emphasis from analyzing individual investments to that of determining the relationships among the investments that comprise the total portfolio. In other words, the investment focus is on the totality of the portfolio and not on the individual investments that make up the portfolio.

Money Market Funds This term refers to mutual funds that invest in low-risk, highly liquid, short-term financial instruments. The net asset value of these funds is kept at $1 per share and the average portfolio maturity is 30 to 60 days. Some money market funds only invest in government securities such as Treasury bills, some only in tax-free securities, while others also invest in securities issued by banks such as bankers acceptances and in securities issued by large corporations such as commercial paper. Money market funds usually pay higher interest rates than regular savings accounts.

Monte Carlo Simulation This is a "what if" tool of statistical analysis that provides a variety of possible outcomes as well as the likelihood that each will occur. *See* pages 224-226 in Chapter 9.

Mortgage Backed Securities Fixed-income investments secured by a pool of mortgages on real estate. *See* Fixed Income.

Municipal Bond A bond that is issued by a state or local government, such as a county or city. Interest on municipal bonds is not subject to federal income tax. Municipal bonds are issued to fund capital improvements such as roads, airports, water districts, libraries and schools. An investor who is a citizen of the state issuing a municipal bond is exempt not only from paying federal income taxes, but also state and local income taxes on the bond's interest payments. Such bonds are therefore favored by high tax-bracket investors. *See* Tax-Free Bond.

Mutual Fund A professionally-managed investment company that commingles money from many investors and buys securities such as stocks, bonds or other securities. The term "mutual" comes from the fact that the shareholders of the fund actually own it. They pay a pro rata share of the mutual fund's annual expenses and obtain a pro rata share of income earned and capital gains realized. An "open-end" mutual fund sells its own new shares to investors and stands ready to buy back its old shares from departing investors. This is the typical mutual fund marketed to investors. "Closed-end" mutual fund shares are transferable in the open market and are bought and sold like shares of individual stocks. There are now over 8,000 mutual funds in existence in the U.S. compared to about 450 in 1976.

NASDAQ (National Association of Securities Dealers Automated Quotation System) A national market for trading stocks. The electronic equivalent of an exchange, it does not have a physical location like the NYSE. Generally, the stocks of smaller companies are traded in this market. However, some very large and well-known companies such as Microsoft and Apple Computer are traded on NASDAQ.

New York Stock Exchange (NYSE) This stock exchange is by far the largest in the U.S. in terms of dollar volume. It is also known as the "Big Board." There are about 2,900 stocks that are listed on this 205-year old exchange. In 1996 an average of over 505 million shares changed hands daily in almost 370,000 trades at a value of over $21 billion per trading day. The total value of all shares traded on the NYSE in 1996 was $1.9 trillion.

Nominal Rate of Return The stated rate of return on an investment that has not been adjusted for inflation or for any other factor such as taxes.

Non-market Risk That portion of total investment risk that can be largely eliminated from a well-diversified portfolio; also called "diversifiable risk." It is risk that is unique to an individual investment.

Over-the Counter (OTC) A market that deals in stocks not listed on the major exchanges or NASDAQ. It is a market made over the telephone or between market dealers who act either as principals or brokers for their clients. Thousands of stocks, mostly representing smaller and newer companies, are traded over-the-counter. The OTC market is also the principal market for U.S. government and municipal bonds.

Owner An investor who owns something rather than lending, usually by investing in stocks or stock mutual funds, but also real estate or a business enterprise. An owner participates in the fortunes—good and bad—of the equity invested in. *See* Equities, Common Stock.

Passive Investing An investment strategy based on the idea that it is unlikely investors can beat the market. Passive investors usually invest in index funds whose performances mimic investment asset classes. These investors don't try to pick stocks or time markets, but just harness the market's movements and the power of compound returns. By doing so, passive investors minimize management costs and taxes. *See* Buy and Hold.

Personal Assets The assets held by an investor outside of any tax-deferred retirement plans such as IRAs, 401(k)s and profit-sharing plans. The investment return of these assets is taxed currently.

Personal Volatility The unpredictable changing events that occur in the lives of investors such as marriage, divorce, family difficulties, health problems, job loss or promotion, depression, loss of a loved one, birth of a child, financial reversals and stress.

Portfolio A collection of investments held by an investor. A portfolio may include only one asset class such as several large company stocks or it could include many asset classes such as stocks, bonds, precious metals and real estate.

Portfolio Design The process of designing a portfolio of investments in a way that is consistent with his or her tolerance for risk and desire for return. Portfolio design consists of three steps. First, decide which specific asset classes of stocks and/or fixed-income investments to include in the portfolio. Second, determine what percentages to invest in each of the selected asset classes. Third, select specific investments within each asset class. Portfolio design is another term for "asset allocation" and greatly influences the investment performance of a portfolio. *See* Asset Allocation.

Portfolio Turnover Rate A measure of the trading activity of a mutual fund which gives an indication of the frequency that securities are bought and sold during the course of a year. For example, a turnover rate of 100% could mean the manager completely replaced the fund's assets during the year. Higher turnover can produce increased costs as well as higher rates of realized capital gains which can result in increased taxes. Portfolio turnover can vary enormously among mutual funds.

Precious Metals Gold, silver, platinum and other investment grade metals. Classified as an equity asset class.

Principal An investment's face value which does not include the interest or dividends that it pays. Commonly, the original amount of money invested in a bond, stock or mutual fund.

Prospectus The document that describes a mutual fund's investment objectives and risks, a listing of its past financial data, a table of fund costs, procedures for buying and selling shares in the mutual fund and a list of its officers and directors. Under the Securities Act of 1933, a prospectus must be supplied to every prospective purchaser of shares in a mutual fund.

Purchasing Power The amount of goods and services that a given amount of money can purchase. Inflation erodes the purchasing power of money. *See* Inflation, Deflation.

Qualified Retirement Plan A retirement plan that is in compliance with the rules and regulations of the Internal Revenue Service. Contributions are usually tax deductible and principal and earnings on these contributions are tax-sheltered until they are withdrawn at retirement or when the investor dies or is disabled.

Real Estate Investment Trust (REIT) REITs hold stocks or bonds of companies that invest in real estate. They invest in properties such as apartment buildings, warehouses, shopping centers and other rental properties. Investors can also buy REITs through mutual funds.

Real Return The stated, nominal rate of return reduced by the rate of inflation. For example, if the nominal rate of return on a certificate of deposit is 6 percent and the inflation rate is 4 percent, then the real return is 2 percent. *See* Inflation, Nominal Rate of Return.

Rebalancing The process of restoring a portfolio to its original asset allocation percentages or portfolio design. As the investments in asset classes in a portfolio appreciate and decline in value, their relative percentage weightings in the portfolio also increase or decrease. By rebalancing, a portfolio is brought back to its original percentage weightings by selling some of the securities that have increased in value and purchasing more of the asset classes that are under weighted.

Recession A period of no growth or slow growth in the economy. In a recession, unemployment increases and business activity decreases.

Risk There are many different kinds of risk and various definitions for it. *See* Standard Deviation, Market Risk, Inflation Risk, Interest Rate Risk, Non-market Risk, Volatility.

Risk-Free Rate of Return Usually refers to the return on 90-day Treasury bills ("T-bills"). A T-bill is used as a proxy to define "no risk" because of its guaranteed repayment by the federal government and short-term maturity. But even short-term securities such as T-bills sometimes carry risk in that they are susceptible to reduction of purchasing power during periods of high inflation.

Risk Premium The expected rate of return above and beyond the risk-free rate of return that investors demand to compensate them for assuming higher risk. For example, a stock's risk premium is the return that a stock may earn in excess of the risk-free rate of return from 90-day Treasury bills.

Risk Tolerance An investor's personal ability or willingness to endure declines in the prices of investments. For many investors there is a big difference between what they *think* is their risk tolerance and what it actually turns out to be.

Securities Any one of various investment choices such as stocks, bonds or mutual funds, etc.

Securities Analyst An individual who is responsible for financial analysis, including research on a company's financial situation to determine its suitability as an investment.

Security Selection An investment strategy which attempts to identify securities that will outperform the market or meet other specific criteria. One variation of this strategy is known as "stock picking" in which the investor attempts to find securities that are "undervalued" and to sell securities (or never buy them) that are "overvalued."

Short-Term Bonds Generally, bonds that have maturities of one to two years.

Small-company Stocks "Small-cap" stocks usually refer to the smallest 20 percent of stocks (in terms of market value) listed on the New York Stock Exchange as well as certain stocks listed on the American Stock Exchange and stocks traded over-the-counter. Frequently defined as stocks that have less than $500 million in total market value. Some small-company stocks pay dividends but not as consistently as large-company stocks because they are growing and usually reinvest most of their earnings in the company's development. Historically, small-cap stocks have produced greater returns with higher volatility than large-cap stocks.

Standard & Poor's 500 Index The composite investment results of 500 companies selected to be a benchmark of large-company U.S. stocks. It includes industrial, utility, financial, and transportation stocks. The S&P 500 is weighted by the market value of the stocks contained in the index. *See* Market Value.

Standard Deviation A statistical calculation used to measure the historical volatility (or up and down fluctuations in market value) of an asset class or individual asset. One standard deviation captures the high and low range of returns two-thirds of the time (while two standard deviations capture the range of returns about 95 percent of the time and three standard deviations about 99 percent of the time). The wider the range of returns, the larger the standard deviation and the greater the volatility.

Statistical History This is a term for the historical performance of different investment asset classes stated in percentages or dollars. For example, the large-company stocks represented by the S&P 500 generated an average annual compound return of 10.7 percent over the 71-year period of 1926 through 1996.

Stock A share of ownership in a corporation and a portion of its profits. *See* Common Stock, Equities.

Tactical Asset Allocation Those who engage in tactical asset allocation typically move assets from what they believe are overvalued areas of the market to undervalued. For example, the manager of a tactical asset allocation fund may reallocate the holdings of the fund according to his or her estimation of the future direction of the economy, shifting from 30 percent stock, 40 percent bond and 30 percent cash to 60 percent stock and 40 percent bond.

Tax-Deferred The ability to accumulate income which is not taxed when earned, but is taxed at some later time when it is withdrawn. Examples of tax-deferred investments are IRA and 401(k) accounts and tax-deferred annuities.

Tax-free Bond A municipal bond whose income is exempt from state and/or federal income taxes. *See* Municipal Bond.

Technical Analysis The analysis of stocks by examining their relative strengths, moving averages, exchange volume figures and patterns on price charts. Some stock pickers use this method of analyzing stocks in attempts to predict the future behavior of certain stocks or groups of stocks. *See* p. 190.

Time-weighted Rate of Return A method of computing the total rate of return of a portfolio. It counts each period equally, and recognizes the effect of cash flows such as new contributions and expenditures.

Total Return The investment return which results from a combination of income (yield) such as interest and dividends from an investment plus the change in value over time (appreciation or depreciation).

Transaction Costs The amount of costs incurred in the purchase and sale of securities, usually due to commissions paid to make the trades.

Treasury Bills (T-Bills) Short-term obligations of the federal government issued for 13, 26 or 52 week periods. T-bills have a minimum face value of $10,000 but are sold at a discount. This means that investors will not receive interest payments. Instead, they pay less than the face value of the Treasury bill and then receive the full face amount when they come due. The difference represents the interest due the investor. Treasury bills are exempt from state and local taxation, and repayment of their principal and interest are guaranteed by the full faith and credit of the United States government. T-bills are often referred to as "risk-free" investments.

Treasury Bonds Obligations of the federal government that are issued for 10, 20 and 30-year terms. Treasury bonds are issued in minimum denominations and interest is paid semi-annually.

Treasury Notes Obligations of the federal government that are issued for periods of from one to ten years. Treasury notes are issued in minimum denominations of $5,000 for those with terms less than four years and $1,000 for terms of 4 to 10 years. They pay interest semi-annually.

Turnover Ratio *See* Portfolio Turnover Rate.

Value Investor An investor who mainly invests in companies believed to be currently undervalued by the market. A value investor purchases companies with price-earning ratios and price-to-book values below the broader market. This style of investing is essentially contrarian because it requires investors to pick stocks that no one else wants to own.

Variable Annuity An investment contract sold by an insurance company which allows the purchaser to invest in mutual funds in a tax-deferred environment. Contributions are unlimited but cannot be deducted from income taxes; earnings accumulate tax-deferred until withdrawn. The term "variable" comes from the fact that the contract value is based on the underlying market value of the assets in the mutual funds (which varies over time). Variable annuities can also include an option that guarantees the return of the original investment amount in the event of the investor's death.

Volatility The sudden, unpredictable up and down price movements of a particular investment. Investments with high volatility are considered to be higher risk investments. Stocks are typically more volatile than bonds in their price movements, but bonds have been known to be even more volatile than stocks at times. A common method of measuring volatility is known as "standard deviation." *See* Standard Deviation.

Wilshire 5000 Equity Stock Index An index created in 1971 that is composed of virtually all stocks in the U.S. stock markets. Currently, this index consists of about 7,500 stocks.

Yield The income portion of investment return, such as the interest rate of a bond or the dividend percent of a stock. Part of the total return of an investment.

INDEX

The Meaning of Success

To laugh often and much;
To win the respect of intelligent people
  and the affection of children;
To earn the appreciation of honest critics
  and endure the betrayal of false friends;
To appreciate beauty;
To find the best in others;
To leave the world a bit better, whether by a healthy child, a
  garden patch, or a redeemed social condition;
To know even one life has breathed easier because you lived...
This is to have succeeded.

— Ralph Waldo Emerson

BRUCE J. TEMKIN, MSPA, EA

Bruce J. Temkin is a nationally recognized educator and authority on retirement and financial decision making and has authored and taught numerous advanced continuing education programs on these subjects. He is also licensed as an Enrolled Actuary. Mr. Temkin has made presentations to national conferences including those sponsored by the American Law Institute-American Bar Association/Stanford Law School, American Institute of Certified Public Accountants, American College of Trust and Estate Council, the International Foundation of Employee Benefit Plans, College for Financial Planning, and Institute of Certified Financial Planners, just to name a few.

Mr. Temkin's ability to translate even the most complex subjects into everyday language and his unique sense of humor have made him a sought-after speaker to business, civic, charitable, professional and financial organizations throughout the United States. He has chaired numerous national programs on the impact of tax reform, and has the distinction of developing the American Law Institute-American Bar Association's national program on financial planning for lawyers and their clients. Recent works include "Creative Distribution Planning from IRAs and Qualified Plans."

Mr. Temkin is frequently quoted in news publications such as *Newsweek, Forbes, The Wall Street Journal, The New York Times* and *Nation's Business*, on a variety of retirement and investment issues. His civic activities include serving on the Board of Directors of the Small Business Council of America and the Center for Infant/Parent Development. Mr. Temkin lives with his wife and son in Studio City, California.

Mr. Temkin acts as a special advisor to Silver Oak Advisory Group and its clients.

Additional copies of this book
may be ordered from:

Fairfield Press
2900 Fourth Street North, Suite A202
St. Petersburg, FL 33704

Phone: 1-888-820-5958
Fax: 1-727-821-1713